DIRTY SECRETS

AN EXPOSE OF ZAMBIA'S UNSPOKEN CULTURAL SKELETONS

CHRISTINE PHIRI MUSHIBWE

AND

MUYEKO ZENAIDA MUSHIBWE

ISBN
Paperback 979-8-89588-344-0
Hardcase 979-8-89610-337-0

Dedication

"Dedicated to all my grandchildren and their children
and their children!"

Contents

Acknowledgement

We would like to acknowledge the countless victims and survivors whose lives have been irrevocably affected by hidden truths. Your experiences and the trauma you've endured are unique and deeply personal. While they can never be fully replicated, your stories will reach thousands, offering inspiration and healing in ways unimaginable. It is through the courage to share these stories that others find the strength and resolve to speak out and share their own journeys. Your voice matters, and its impact cannot be overstated.

Thank you for your bravery to speak out.

We also give all glory and honour to the source of knowledge and wisdom, our Almighty God. For this, we are truly grateful.

Lastly, we extend our sincere thanks to every reader of this book. Your decision to engage with these pages will not be regretted. Thank you for choosing to read this book.

About the Book

The book aims to shed light on the lives destroyed by secrets individuals are forced to keep to maintain appearances, protect their families, or preserve cultural norms. Real stories from real people are provided under pseudonyms for protection and confidentiality.

As authors, we are cognizant of the sentiments and triggers that may arise due to the content of this book. However, at the heart of this book is the truth. Truth should never be compromised or traded for anything.

This book serves as an important documentation of significant insights into core issues that our culture tends to perpetuate in the name of preserving certain practices. These practices have caused untold misery to many unsuspecting victims.

While culture is inherently good and not all its practices are evil or bad, this book does not call for people to discard everything indiscriminately. Instead, it advocates for identifying better methods of preserving valuable aspects of our culture while discarding those that are harmful. What is retained should protect and benefit everyone, contributing to the betterment of our society. It has been said that people create culture, not the other way around. Therefore, we owe it to ourselves and to past and future generations to do better—to create a culture that preserves what is important and eliminates what is redundant and destructive.

The concern lies in practices that continue to destroy innocent lives. These practices have a tendency to protect and glorify the villain while the victim is left to live with pain, shame, and deprivation. Because trauma is not visible, no pain is observable, the victim is overlooked and any complaint of how they are feeling watered down or reduced to not being strong or being a weakling. Meanwhile, the villain moves on, while the victim is shattered for life, forced to keep a secret that is re-experienced daily with immense pain.

Note that some stories included in the book are the experiences of the authors. All narratives were willingly provided, with the owners consenting to share their stories under the condition that their real names are withheld. Hence, all names of the victims and places are pseudonyms.

Illusions!

Pretty as a picture.

Passed down from my ancestors, like an heirloom. My mother wore it so well while my father carried it with a silent dignity. Once in a while, we could see the illusion slip, but it would so quickly be put back in place you would wonder if what you had just seen was a shift in the light.

As we grew, as children do, imagination and curiosity bloomed. We questioned everything, with the innocence of children, but we quickly hit the ceiling as our parents must have done and as their parents before them did. "Hush child, we don't talk about that!" "This is how it has always been done!" "This is who we are, who you are! You will be smart to fall in line".

With every roadblock, the bright sunlight of childhood was dimmed with the understanding that with maturity and adulthood, came the grey skies. Just like Joseph with his coat of many colours, we got given our coat of illusions. Save face. Till we lost our individual identity. We learned like millions before us, to take it on the chin, that holding our breath was better and safer than exhaling and breathing. Despite the heavy coat that curved our backs in pain, we were to bear its weight willingly, and we were applauded for being so brave, so strong.

We learned to embody the illusion. Watch your mouth, mind your manners, people are coming over, hide the tear stains, put on a smile, you are not the first to go through it and you won't be the last, just make sure the Jenga pieces don't all come falling down after you touch them. That's about right, straight back, straight shoulders. So here we stand, like statues in a burning building. We have mastered the illusion well. So well that we can breathe through the smoke and pretend the air is just fresh, no one questions why we are here, why the building is on fire, or who set it or why we don't try to put out the flames or get out. Once in a while we hear the screams of anguish but that's no business of ours. Loud and powerful are the voices that silence the screams! What are you doing? This is our lot, this is how it's been, how it's meant to be, and how it's always going to be.

Sometimes I wonder... Would we recognise ourselves? Would anyone else? If we all took off the illusion? If we refused to pretend. Truth is, I hate this coat. I really do, but it has become my identity. It is not only part of me but expected of me. Besides, I have had it for so long and I look so darn good in it.

Introduction

Secrets. Defined as "kept hidden or separate from the knowledge of others."

Everyone has a secret, or secrets. Some we share with a select, elite few, while others we keep to ourselves. It often takes years before those hidden truths clamour for release, and when they finally spill out, they may be so old that they crumble into nothingness, blown away like dust in the wind. Other secrets are buried so deeply that we carry them to our graves. Although the old adage says we die alone, ironically, our secrets sometimes remain our companions even in death. We hold onto them not only out of loyalty, but also because we know that once revealed, the damage may be irreparable.

What makes a secret dirty? How does it transition from innocent to sinister? Merriam-Webster defines a dirty secret as "something bad that someone does not want people to know."[1] Collins dictionary defines secret as "kept hidden or separate from the knowledge of others."[2]

We live in a world governed by an "I don't ask, and you don't tell" mentality. We all see the signs and hear the unspeakable horrors, but as long as we don't ask, no one feels compelled to tell. Even if they do, often nothing substantial is done about it. While secrets themselves can be harmless, when they mask traumas, they don't simply disappear—they metastasise. Unhealed trauma

---

[1] Merriam-Webster.com Dictionary, Merriam-Webster, https://www.merriam-webster.com/dictionary/dirty%20little%20secret. Accessed 2 Apr.2022

[2] Collins English Dictionary and Thesaurus, 21st Century Edition

can pass down through generations, impacting everything we do, touch, and become.

Everyone has secrets; every family, community, society, and nation has secrets. Sometimes, these secrets are so ingrained in our way of life that they become mistaken as integral to our identity. Speaking out against them or shedding light on them can be met with resistance, perceived as an attack on the people rather than on the issue itself.

It has been said that people create culture, not the other way around. While this notion works seamlessly in theory, it often fails in practice. Secrets, when they are traumas in disguise, perpetuate cycles of pain and suffering that need to be addressed for the betterment of individuals and society as a whole.

Dirty Secrets!

Behind Closed Doors

Many of us are familiar with the saying, "don't air out your dirty linen in public." This phrase, common across various cultures and countries, carries a uniform meaning: it suggests that problems should be kept private and resolved internally. While the saying "don't air out your dirty linen in public" holds some wisdom, there are times when it is necessary to bring these issues to light to provide justice and closure for the victim. Certain problems need to be aired publicly to prevent further harm. The longer these issues remain hidden, the worse the situation becomes.

Home[3] is meant to be a place of refuge, a sanctuary where we feel safe. But what happens when home becomes the very place where the monsters reside? Or where the monsters, if not permanent residents, visit frequently and are even honoured guests? A place where these monsters dominate and have free rein? There comes a point in time—and indeed in history—when airing out one's dirty linen becomes the only way to achieve change, healing, and reconciliation. This is the aim of this book.

Our purpose is not to expose these stories for profit or popularity but rather to shine a light on these dirty secrets that continue to weigh heavily on victims and survivors, even after many years. We seek to provide relief to these individuals so they can move forward.

The desire to write this book was born out of a conversation I had with my daughters, as is our custom. To talk freely

---

[3] Home for the purposes of this book is used broadly, alluding to the physical home, as well as to one's place of residence.

about any subject in life. Talking about secrets, I narrated to her about a near rape I had as a child. During our discussions, we addressed many issues, some of which are included in this book. This conversation marked the genesis of this book, "Dirty Secrets!"

As parents, my husband and I understood that among the many challenges of raising children, one of the heaviest responsibilities is preparing them to face a world that will inevitably burden them with secrets we do not want them to have, but cannot entirely shield them from. We wanted our children to understand that keeping such secrets is harmful. We wanted them to be wiser than we were, never to bear the pain and burden of keeping a dirty secret.

Our hope is that you read this book with an open mind, free from prejudices, judgements, and preconceived notions. We want you to reflect on the issues we raise, do your homework, and critically assess them for yourself. Then, join us in taking a stand against practices that do not benefit us as a people. Don't just take our word for it; investigate and engage with the content. Together, we can work towards making Zambia the great nation it has the potential to be, passing down not the traumas we have failed to address in our lifetime, but a legacy of healing and progress for those who come after us.

After experiencing sexual harassment, assault, violence, or abuse, individuals often encounter a universal pressure to remain silent. They are silenced or made to feel ashamed and filled with guilt. This guilt or shame can stem from various sources: those who were supposed to protect them but didn't, the environment, society, or even themselves. Various authors, scholars, and psychologists offer different reasons for why this occurs. However, one consistent truth is that after such a violation—whether physical, psychological, or emotional—there is an overwhelming sense of shame. Even if it is a near attack, a feeling of being violated occurs. Something has happened. Something has been taken or stolen. Even when words fail to adequately describe the experience or articulate the emotions felt, the sense of violation remains.

For some, the perpetrator or abuser will swear them to secrecy through threats or shame, using whatever means are most effective. If the incident involves family members, close friends, or neighbours, a family may decide to sweep everything under the carpet. They may hope that by not addressing the issue, both the victim and the perpetrator will somehow be protected and move past the experience. Society and culture often play a significant role in perpetuating the dirty secret and ensuring its continued custody, even when the perpetrator does not explicitly threaten the victim into silence. Listen to the account below.

Anca's Story

I was coming home from school one afternoon. My stop was the last one, so I preferred to sit right at the back and took the window seat. I had taken off my tie as it was hot and unbuttoned the first 3 buttons. I was a late bloomer and barely had any breasts per se. They were there, but you could easily miss them. The bus had just about filled up, and I was daydreaming when this man stuck his hand through the window and down my shirt, popping an extra button. I was startled as I felt his hand on my flesh. I reacted and slammed the window, jamming his hand as his hand came out of my shirt, and he quickly tried to pull his hand away. He, in pain, cried out, and this alerted the rest of the passengers on the bus. As the bus slowly tried to pull away from the station, the man's shout stopped it. He was swearing at me, calling me names, but my hand was still pulling the window towards me, trapping his hand. The man next to me reached over and pulled my hand off the window and released the man's hand. The driver was yelling back, asking what was going on, and the conductor trying to make sense of what was happening over the noise in the bus was equally wondering why I had trapped a man's hand in the window. The man who was beside me was saying he had not seen a thing and did not know why I had done what I had done or if the man was a thief. Finally, a woman in front of me asked me what had happened, and I said, "he put his hand in my shirt and touched my breast." I don't know what I had expected, but at my response, some people laughed, others sighed, and the conductor sucked his teeth at me. The woman looked disbelievingly at me and said out loud, "mami, you almost broke a man's hand because he touched you?!" All the passengers left at that. The bus left the station, and I was the main topic of discussion as we drove stop after stop. Jokes were told, others laughed, the man who had leaned across to release the man's hand told me there would come a day I would wish men tried to touch my breasts. I sat quietly in my seat, wishing the ground would open up beneath me. Like I said, my stop was the last one; I had to endure a 30-plus ride, and every time a person got on the bus and asked what the excitement was about, they were told my story. I learned something of the society we live in on that day.

Such an experience illustrates how instances of crying out, "I am violated," are often trivialised. In this case, the victim cried out because a man violated her in broad daylight and in public. However, instead of receiving support, her reaction was unsupported, and the violator received sympathy.

Why is There a Lack of Data on This?

When it comes to abuse, whether sexual or otherwise, it is evident that we, as a country, have insufficient data on the subject. Arguably, this is because the vast majority of incidents are never reported. Others may be reported initially but are later retracted. Of the few cases that are reported and remain un-retracted, little is often done in the name of justice for the survivors of horrific abuse. In short, perpetrators and abusers frequently continue with their lives free of any consequences, while victims are left to pick up the pieces of their shattered lives, receiving little to no help for the trauma they have endured.

Unfortunately, in Zambia—and probably across much of Africa—society plays a significant role in silencing victims, thereby empowering abusers. The reality is that a perpetrator will not recognise the error of their ways by going unpunished. Although there are exceptions, these should not be mistaken for the rule.

If you sit down with a group of women, the majority, if not all, will recount an "incident" that happened to them. Probe further, and they will admit to carrying a secret, often imploring you not to say a word. If permission is granted to use their story, they will ask that their names remain concealed. While privacy concerns are valid, the underlying reason is that the act remains a dirty secret meant to protect the abuser. This issue is not limited to women. If you ask men the same question, some will admit that something happened to them as well, particularly during childhood. However, few will openly discuss these experiences. Our society does not permit such topics to be discussed openly, and when discussions do occur, they almost always exclude men and boys.

This societal norm prevents individuals from speaking up, leading them to keep the incident a secret against all odds. To explore how our society enables the keeping of these dirty secrets, we will delve deeper into this issue in the next chapter.

Stolen

It's the feeling you cannot get rid of,

The stain that refuses to go away,

It's silence so loud,

The foreboding feeling of a violation occurred,

Of something having been taken from you;

Yet, there is nothing you can say or do about it,

You may try, but you and I both know the reality.

We can see the outcome; we have seen the outcomes:

They will say it's your fault; it's always your fault.

You should have known better;

It's not always in the words,

It's in the stares, the murmurs, the ostracisation,

It's a second violation of your soul,

Society will kneel beside you as you bleed out on the floor,

Hand you the bloody knife and carefully place it beside you
silently.

You will know then what so many of us have learned the hard way,

As you hear the fateful words that have been passed down
from generation to generation,

This time you will carry them as your own...

"Look what you made *him* do? It's all your fault."

Society

Those who are able to see beyond the shadows

and lies of their culture will never be understood let alone

believed by the mass – Plato

Society is an integral aspect of human existence. Though its exact origin is debatable, it is evident that no one lives outside a society, and no society exists without people. The coming together of individuals from different backgrounds gives birth to a society. These individuals unite for various reasons, and living together harmoniously demands finding common ground due to differing perceptions of life shaped by their diverse backgrounds. In simple terms, society is a group of individuals who come together and interact directly or indirectly with one another. The behaviour patterns that emerge among these people are distinct, giving the society its uniqueness and distinguishing it from others in both nature and practice. These individuals develop local knowledge and understanding of things typical to their environment.

Society cannot be discussed devoid of culture and traditions. They are like a three-strand cord, intertwined and qualifying each other. Society and culture have an intricate relationship, and it is easy to confuse the 2, thinking they are the same. Culture can be considered a by-product of the society in which it operates. It encompasses the complex learned behaviour patterns of people living in a particular society. Mushibwe (2014, p. 24) posits that culture can be "defined as the personality and the heartbeat of a society, which gives an individual his/her cultural identity."

It is the totality of everyday life, including knowledge, norms, beliefs, values, customs, language, habits, and skills, that enables individuals to relate to others in society. People belonging to the same culture may interpret the world in roughly the same ways and express their thoughts and feelings similarly.

Every society on earth has its own culture that makes it distinctive and separate from others. Culture is a powerful tool people use to survive in their society and live harmoniously. It is meant to serve as a unifying factor, fostering unity and giving identity to a society. As people interact, a culture evolves through the traditions practiced, helping them live harmoniously across generations. The codes that unify them are well explained and well kept, and going against these codes raises strong defence from loyal custodians. "This cannot go out," the custodians argue, for then the society's "innocent" image is exposed.

To this day, certain topics remain taboo and are not discussed openly. Sex, along with all related topics, is one such taboo. It is considered a private act that enjoys privacy at all costs, and its intricacies should not be shared. While there is nothing inherently wrong with maintaining privacy, the contention arises when secrecy is demanded in the context of sexual assault or molestation. When an assault is shrouded in secrecy, the individual is left at a loss, unsure of what to do or whom to turn to. The insistence on secrecy protects the perpetrator and perpetuates the trauma of the victim. This demand for silence leaves victims isolated and unsupported, unable to seek justice or healing. Those in whom the victim manages to share the incident often reinforce secrecy and assure the victim that time will heal the wounds. Yet still, others are also victims who may have tried to speak out but were undignifiedly silenced. The silencing itself leads to further trauma, shame, name-calling, and isolation. Hence, comfort is found in remaining quiet, perpetuating the cycle where victims are told to "keep it to yourself" as a means of safety or protection. This phenomenon occurs because those expected to help may instead support the perpetrator to preserve family or societal image.

Therefore, by bringing these issues to light, we can challenge the cultural norms that enable such secrecy and work towards a society that supports victims and holds perpetrators accountable.

Mina's Story

I was almost raped at 17 years old by my teacher who called me to his house to pick up documents he claimed were important to help me pass my examination. Who wouldn't go for such documents? I was at a boarding school, and the teacher's compound was out of bounds, but as a class monitor, he enabled me to get to the compound. He opened the door at my knock and asked me in. As I walked in, he was behind the door. He closed the door and asked me to sit down. When I looked up, did I realise that I had walked myself into danger. He had no shirt on. I quickly reminded him of my purpose for the visit. He instead asked me questions about who my boyfriend was. I was not interested, but he kept guessing, naming the boys in my class who were just friends. He then stood up and went to a bedroom where some soft music had been playing all the time, and somehow, the music stopped. He had left the door open and then started calling me. I didn't know what to do. I went, 'sir', and he then called me to the bedroom. I slowly stood up and walked to the door, peeked inside and said, "I can't come into your bedroom, sir. I want to go if you do not have the documents." At that, he rushed to where I stood and got hold of me, trying to get me into the bedroom. I held onto the door frame with my life, shouting, "No, sir, please no, please let me go." He instead pulled his face towards mine, trying to kiss me. I turned away from him each time he tried to put his lips on mine. He then leaned on me so hard, almost suffocating me and then stopped trying. I pushed him away with all my strength, and he fell down. I rushed to the main door, and it was locked. "Sit down," he said from the floor. "I haven't even done anything, and you are all panicked." He stood up, and his trousers were wet. He somehow had ejaculated. He unlocked the door, opened it and said before letting me go, "You are an intelligent girl. I don't want you to stop working hard in class. Besides, I have not done anything to you, have I? I also do not want to hear anything about this from anyone. Please, this is between you and me." I walked out silently, and once outside, I ran to the dormitories. I had to face this teacher for the rest of that year as he taught me 2 subjects. I only managed to tell my closest friend who was waiting to see these important documents I had been called for. Since there were no documents, I shared the ordeal and insisted it should be kept a secret because it was demanded.

Our society places a significant emphasis on respecting all adults, a respect often expressed through obedience to our elders. However, this obedience sometimes comes at a great cost to the individual, particularly the most vulnerable and disadvantaged, who may not fully comprehend the consequences. Research shows that most abuse is carried out by someone close to the victim, and despite our limited data, this is the case we face here in Zambia.

Our culture, society, and traditions create a fertile and conducive playground for abusers who exploit these dynamics with barely restrained abandon. An abuser can "groom" a potential victim for days, weeks, months, or even years before making their move, at which point the victim is ensnared in the web of deceit.

How Society Accommodates, Perpetuates, or Promotes the Dirty Secret

Grooming

Grooming is a term not widely used or acknowledged in our society, but this does not mean it is absent. Kenneth Lanning is credited with being one of the first to use the term "grooming." His major thesis explains the impact on victims, particularly their compliance with the offender. This conceptualisation helps educate the public about the complex reactions during and after the event, as most of our knowledge is derived post-abuse.

Lanning's conclusion emphasises that the nature and development of the relationship between the abused and the abuser is more important than the specific act of seduction or grooming.

Lanning's concept of "grooming" accurately reflects the process by which some sex offenders non-violently access and control their child victims to facilitate sexual victimisation. However, he notes that threats and force are still most often employed in cases involving strangers. Sexual assault has evolved, and it's not always the stereotypical 'stranger danger' scenario. Grooming is usually nonviolent, making it easier for perpetrators to gain access to victims, allowing the abuse to go undetected for extended periods due to the victim's compliance. Furthermore, groomers often cloak their actions with statements like "I am doing this because I love you," "I care for you," "You are special to me," or "You are my favourite." They may also use gifts as a way to reinforce silence or their purported affectionate intentions.

According to Lanning, there is much confusion and disagreement over the precise meaning of the term grooming. He advises that anyone using the term must clearly define it and consistently use their definition. For the purposes of our book, we will define grooming as techniques used by an abuser to manipulate a potential victim into compliance and even agreement with their own abuse, significantly decreasing the risk of discovery and maintaining the secrecy of the abuse.

Grooming is a form of control. A relationship or acquaintance is forged over time, with the perpetrator lowering the victim's inhibitions, gaining their trust, and most importantly, their loyalty and access. When abuse occurs, inappropriate behaviours have been normalised and desensitised for the victim, who may see these behaviours as acceptable. Grooming applies to both children and adults.

The grooming process makes the victim feel complicit in their violation or even as if they consented. Blackmail often plays a significant role in ensuring the dirty secret is kept. The victim remains unaware of the manipulation they have undergone and that abuse was always the intended outcome. An abuser adapts their techniques depending on the potential victim, portraying themselves as a nice guy, favourite one, confidant, friend, empathetic shoulder, giver of gifts, etc. Even when the victim is no longer under the direct control of the abuser, the dirty secret is kept due to confusion, fear, shame, or guilt. Moreover, living in a society that blames victims does not help either.

What are we saying, our society's emphasis on respect and obedience, combined with cultural norms and traditions, creates an environment that enables grooming and abuse. This perpetuates a cycle of silence and secrecy, protecting abusers and leaving victims isolated and unsupported. Addressing these issues openly and redefining societal attitudes towards abuse and grooming is essential for protecting the vulnerable and ensuring justice and healing for victims.

Awii's Story

When I was 8 years old, I had this experience I have never forgotten. A relative of my father visited us as a family. He was married and he had children my age. For most of the time, he called me his beautiful princess. I loved it. He would hug me, lift me up and swing me each time I walked into the lounge. He would give me sweets even when my mum insisted not to. When in the lounge, I would sit next to him and he would slip sweets to me so my mother would not see. One evening, he came and sat next to me while I was watching TV. My mum and dad had gone out, leaving me in his care. I comfortably snuggled into him. Suddenly, he started touching me. I was uncomfortable and panicked but he told me that it was okay. It is just a game we are going to play. I trusted him. Yes, I did and I sat there as he put his hand in my underwear. He was 'touching me.' I began crying silently, not knowing what to say. I was uncomfortable but kept saying, "Quiet!" in a hushed voice. He put my hand on his manhood. He looked into my eyes and said, "You see, it is just a game my beautiful princess. Stop crying, will you?" Then there was a sound of the gate opening. It was my mum and dad coming back. "Look at me, if you tell your mum, you will regret this. I will tell her you asked me to touch you. This is our game and it should not be shared with anyone. Dry your tears," he said as he dashed out to his bedroom. I pulled myself together. Dried my tears and lay down on the sofa pretending I was asleep as mum walked in through the door.

Victim-Blaming

Victim-blaming is a pervasive cultural phenomenon where abuse, though abhorred in theory, is often normalised, excused, or even justified by blaming the victim for their own mistreatment. Victim-blaming rationalises violence by blaming the victim for their own mistreatment. For example, the story above is one such situation. The uncle blames the girl for touching him. This cultural environment can be observed in the objectification of women, their bodies, and the language used, leading to a society indifferent to women's rights and safety.

In our Zambian society, while abuse in all its forms—physical, sexual, psychological—is theoretically condemned, it is tacitly tolerated in reality. This contradiction becomes evident when speaking with individuals who will readily recount experiences of abuse they have faced. Despite these experiences, societal norms make it difficult for victims to speak out. Furthermore, the burden of proof often rests on the victim, making it challenging to convince others that a crime has occurred. This marginalisation of victims reinforces the manipulative tactics abusers use to maintain control, convincing victims that they are to blame for the violence inflicted upon them.

In theory and in abstract terms, most abuse - physical, sexual, psychological, etc. - is a crime that is abhorred by our Zambian society, culture, and traditions. However, this is tolerated in reality. It does not take much to prove this fact. Just ask any woman in your life if she has faced any of the above-mentioned abuses, and she will confirm it with you.

In a notable incident from 2020 reported by the Daily Mail on June 7th, a 19-year-old student jumped from an apartment building while trying to escape an alleged rape, resulting in broken limbs. The response from society to this tragic event was disheartening, reflecting victim-blaming attitudes. See below some of the captured questions and claims.

- ➤ Victim's actions where blamed as the cause of the assault: Questions like "What was she doing with the man alone in the building?" where asked.

- ➤ Attributing the Incident to a Lesson the victim had to learn: Statements such as, "This has now taught her a lesson" implying that the victim's suffering was somehow deserved or necessary as a learning curve.

- ➤ Her behaviour was criticised: Comments such as "Girls of nowadays don't know how to stay put" and "You visit a man who isn't your brother, what do you expect?" Such a comment reinforces stereotypes with implications that the victim's behaviour invited the assault.

- ➤ The Validity of Rape was questioned: Doubts were expressed with statements like "Is that rape sure ... just say you were caught in the very act then you cried rape!" Such a statement undermines the seriousness of the victim's experience.

Impact of Victim-Blaming

Such attitudes within a particular society prevent abusers from being held accountable because they undermine the recognition of abuse as a systemic issue. Instead, victims are led to believe they were somehow responsible for the abuse they suffered. Victim-blaming serves 2 main purposes in society: firstly, it maintains a false facade that bad things only happen to people who deserve them, thus upholding a positive view of the broader society. Secondly, it serves as a cautionary tale to others, promoting a false sense of security that one can avoid harm by adhering to certain behavioural norms (e.g., not drinking, dressing modestly).

We emphasise that victim-blaming perpetuates a distorted view of a just world and fosters a sense of false security, contributing to a culture where victims of abuse are silenced and justice is elusive. Addressing victim-blaming requires challenging deep-seated cultural norms and educating the public on the realities of abuse and its impact on victims.

Victim-blaming sentiments come in many forms, such as:Victim-blaming wears many faces. It can be outright and overt, subtle, or even unconscious, reflecting societal attitudes. It surfaces whenever the default question posed to the victim focuses on what they could have done differently to prevent the abuse, thus placing the blame on them. Some argue that victim-blaming is a psychologically natural reaction to a crime, rooted in society's distorted or mythological view of what a rapist or abuser looks like. This view holds that the perpetrator couldn't be someone familiar, such as an uncle or cousin. Society often expects the abuser to be a stranger, but this is not always the case. The adage "stranger danger" overlooks the fact that many victims face threats from those within their own homes, labelled as father or mother, grandfather or grandmother, brother or sister, uncle or aunt, cousin, etc.

It is time to wake up and face the truth. The monster is not always outside; often, the monster is inside the house, familiar and trusted. In many cases, the abuser is someone well known to the victim, much like the tale of Little Red Riding Hood[4] that teaches children to never trust strangers. The monster no longer hides in the shadows; it has a familiar face and name. "A wolf in sheep's clothing."

---

[4] A fairy European story that dates back to several pre-pre-17th century. It is a fairy tale about a young girl and a sly wolf. https://learnenglishkids.britishcouncil.org/en/short-stories/little-red-riding-hood @British Council, 2017.

Victim-blaming fundamentally reflects society's failure to show empathy. We struggle to accept that someone we know—a brother, a sister, friend, neighbour, work colleague, pastor, etc.—could be a rapist or molester because the realisation is too horrifying to bear. Instead, we speculate about what the victim should have done differently. We might say, "You should have avoided that person because they had an unhealthy attraction to you." Onlookers, observers, and analysts often appear to have more wisdom about an event than the actors involved, and there is a good reason for this. They are in a calm position, with their adrenaline and thinking capacity intact, unclouded by a life-threatening situation. This allows them to analyse the situation and propose the best escape solutions. However, this perspective fails to recognise that no one asks for or deserves abuse, violence, or assault. Further, the inability of those in the midst of a threatening situation to establish the best escape route should not be criticised. While some may manage to escape, not everyone can do so through a well-established route. Each individual's response to a crisis is unique, influenced by the intense pressure and fear they experience. This recognition underscores the importance of understanding and empathy rather than judgement.

Abuse and violence shatter lives, leaving victims with lingering trauma and humiliation. The impact of unwanted touch, groping, sexual violence, harassment, and abuse endures long after the initial act. Yet, when such incidents are raised, the questions asked are often victim-focused, such as "What were you wearing?" "What were you doing there?" "What time was it?" "Were you drunk?" This focus fails to condemn the violation and instead tends to place fault on the victim.

Society has a responsibility to support victims and hold abusers accountable. We must recognise that abuse is a conscious decision made by the abuser, and the only person who can stop abuse is the abuser themselves. Abuse stems from an abuser's sense of entitlement to act as they please, regardless of the harm caused and on whom they act upon. It is essential to shift our perspective and understand that the responsibility for abuse lies solely with the abuser, not the victim, not the environment, not what the victim is wearing nor the size or age. It is a deep-seated state that should be dealt with.

Victim-blaming is a double-edged sword. On one hand, it retraumatises victims and sends a clear message to other victims that they, too, must have done something to warrant the abuse. On the other hand, it fails to hold abusers fully accountable for their actions. This partial accountability empowers abusers, making them feel invincible and unlikely to change their behaviour. The probability of them repeating the offence is high, leading to more abuse and more victims.

Victim-blaming makes it more difficult for victims to speak out and report assaults. This results in fewer reported crimes and even fewer prosecutions. It creates a vicious cycle where victims no longer see the point in reporting attacks because they are likely to be disbelieved, shamed, or made to feel responsible for the abuse. When society turns a blind eye to abusive behaviour, it reinforces and implicitly communicates that nothing unacceptable has occurred, perpetuating the cycle of abuse.

Redundant Laws and Beliefs

Sexual violence and assault are global problems that affect people indiscriminately. While it is a prevalent and persistent issue for women and girls, it is not an exclusively female problem. Many men and boys also face assault, abuse, and violence, although these cases are often underreported. The misconception that women are not capable of committing such crimes contributes to this silence. The truth is, abusiveness is not gender-specific; both men and women can be perpetrators.

In our society, traditional gender roles often define womanhood as submissive and sexually passive, while manhood is characterised as dominant and sexually aggressive. This makes it less believable for men to report sexual assault and violence. When men do speak out, it is more often believed if the perpetrator is male. However, male-on-male assault and violence also go largely unreported due to the stigma associated with it.

Additionally, the legal framework often fails to recognise the nuances of sexual violence against men. For example, male-on-male sexual violence may not be classified as rape but rather as sodomy or non-consensual buggery, particularly in regions where sex between males is illegal and considered unnatural. This legal distinction distorts the boundaries between consensual and non-consensual acts.

There is also an unspoken belief that male-on-male sexual violence and assault only apply to gay men. Victims often fear being labelled as homosexual, which carries further stigmatisation and ostracisation. Furthermore, there is a pervasive belief that men and boys cannot be victims of sexual abuse or violence. This is reflected in laws that typically only address sexual violence against women by men. For instance, rape legislation in some countries, like Zambia, does not apply to men. These laws, and the societal attitudes they reflect, fail to acknowledge female-on-female and female-on-male sexual assault and violence.

Men face similar barriers as women when it comes to reporting sexual assault. They fear disbelief, shame, and being blamed. Common responses to male sexual assault reports include, "Real men cannot get raped," "He probably liked it and enjoyed himself", "He asked for it" or "Only weak men get raped." These responses further discourage men from speaking out and contribute to the underreporting of male sexual violence.

To address these issues, it is crucial to challenge and change the redundant laws and beliefs that perpetuate these harmful stereotypes. Society must recognise that sexual violence and abuse can affect anyone, regardless of gender, and ensure that all victims are supported and believed. Laws must be updated to provide protection and justice for all victims, and societal attitudes must shift to end the stigma surrounding male sexual assault.

Nonetheless, despite women and men facing similar barriers, there are many who posit that male victims/survivors of assault or violence actually encounter further gender-specific barriers.[5] The reasoning behind this argument lies in the fact that men are expected to adhere to the masculine norms that are heavily dependent on men being stoic, resilient, independent, and invulnerable.[6]

Male sexual assault and violence are hardly, if ever, discussed. As a result, men lack reference points and support networks that can provide meaningful assistance. Society's perception of men as the stronger sex contributes to the discomfort around acknowledging male victimhood. The notion of a man being violated challenges deeply ingrained beliefs about masculinity. Men are expected to be strong and masculine, and the idea that they could be raped or assaulted is often repulsive to societal norms. This discomfort leads to a lack of recognition and acknowledgement of male sexual assault and violence. Consequently, victims, both male and female, often do not receive the help they need, and the crime continues to devastate lives while society turns a blind eye.

Another significant deterrent for men in reporting assault or violence is the treatment of other victims, particularly women, in the media. Negative responses such as victim-blaming, disbelief, and ridicule serve as powerful deterrents. Men see how women are treated when they report such crimes and fear receiving the same or worse treatment.

---

[5] B.kenneth Widanaralalage, Benjamine A. Hine, Anthony D. Murphy & Karim Murji (2022) "I Didn't Feel I was a Vicitm":A Phenomenological Analysis of the Experience of Male-on-male Survivors of Rape and Sexual Abuse, Victims & Offenders, DOI:10.1080/15564886.2022.206 9898

[6] Addis, M.E., & Mahalik, J.R. (2003). Men, Masculinty and The Contexts of Help Seeking. American Psychologist, 58(1), 5. https://doi.org/10.1037/0003-066x.58.1.5 [Crossref],[PubMed],[Web of Science(R)],[Google Scholar]

This contrasts with the situation for women, as female sexual assault and violence are more readily acknowledged and accepted in society. Consequently, women have more access to support services and resources, whereas men often find themselves isolated and unsupported in their experiences of sexual violence.

Javaid[7] argues that a man's self-perception is often severely impacted due to a sense of failure for not being 'man enough' during an attack. This can make it extremely difficult for male victims to disclose their experiences or seek help, as they fear further compromising their societal standing. It is important to note that male sexual assault and violence, whether physical, emotional, sexual, or psychological, is neither rare nor a novel issue arising from the increasing legalisation of homosexuality or the broader acceptance of the Lesbian, Gay, Bisexual, Transgender and Queer (LGBTQ) community. This problem has long been present but continually gets swept under the rug to maintain a disguise of moral uprightness, resulting in the issue never being adequately addressed.

The adage "out of sight, out of mind" applies all too well to sexual assault and violence, acting like a cancer that destroys from within. There is an urgent need for greater social awareness of male assault and violence. Recognising that these issues affect men too, and providing appropriate support and resources, is essential for addressing this hidden epidemic.

---

7. Javaid, A (2015). The dark side of men: The nature is Masculinity and its Uneasy Relationship with Male Rape. The Journal of Men's Studies, 23(3), 271-292 https://doi.org/10.1177/1060826515600656 [Crossref],[Google Scholar]

– 04 –

Family Lines

"Don't tell lies."

We hear this over and over growing up. Why?

Because lying is bad. But then, as we grow, we find that lies have different colours,

So now I tell a million lies in order to survive.

I am so good at telling lies. I don't know where to draw the line. I guess I get it from my mother's side.

"Protect the family line!"

Let family secrets remain in the family. Why?

Because exposing them does not make you honest; it opens your family line to destruction.

So now I do all it takes to shield the line.

I am so good at making excuses, I don't know where to draw the line. I guess I get it from my father's side.

"Grow Up"

As we grow into adulthood, we try to outrun the truth,

We have played our roles; we have told lies, protected the family line at all costs.

But we have spent so much time playing pretend.

We forgot that the child within us is still lost, hurt, still a child.

I guess in this way I am my parents' child, because like them, I find we can't outgrow, protect or hide from my family lies.

Broken Moral Fabric

The moral fabric of a society is seen as its cornerstone because it provides and enshrines the standard dignity of its people. This foundation weaves together societal values and morals, creating a cohesive and harmonious community.

In any society, people need control and guidance to maintain harmony, a role typically fulfilled by leaders. Rules and regulations serve as a framework for behavioural patterns, ensuring that individuals can live well together. These rules often emerge in response to new challenges that the society collectively faces. Traditions are formulated to help counter and overcome these challenges, providing stability and continuity.

While traditions are constructed by the members of a given society, they often include elements of inherited cultural characteristics that persist despite changes. Some traditions encourage and foster good behavioural patterns that help bind society together. Additionally, certain traditions and customs are carry-overs from previous societies from which members might have originated. These traditions may be modified or abandoned for the sake of unity, while others evolve through daily interactions among members. New traditions also emerge in response to the everyday challenges people face in their new societal context.

Over time, these traditions take on the weight of law within the society. Breaching these traditions can have severe consequences, ranging from heavy fines to expulsion or ostracism from the community. Thus, traditions and customs play a crucial role in maintaining the moral and social order, ensuring that society remains cohesive and functional.

Society's gatekeepers range from na Chimbusa,[8] shi Chimbusa, elders, and leaders. The moral fabric of society is maintained by gatekeepers who ensure that cultural traditions are disseminated through various forums and that punishment is meted out for violations accordingly. Hierarchies in society play a significant role in maintaining order as they help enforce these traditions and norms. However, the maintenance of this moral fabric can be secretive, mystical, and even vindictive. Fear, whether based on truth, facts, myths, or superstition, often inspires adherence to these traditions.

Society deals ruthlessly with those who contravene cultural expectations. Exclusion from society can be either virtual or physical. Physical exclusion involves expelling the offender from the community, while virtual exclusion entails barring individuals from participating in societal events such as ceremonies and initiations. For example, hierarchical expectations dictate that married elders and individuals of good standing should be sources of wisdom for the young. However, if these individuals are virtually excluded, they lose their prestige and influence. To prevent disgrace and maintain inclusivity, individuals often comply with societal expectations.

Despite these rigid structures, there are instances where the standing of certain individuals in society is questionable, yet their failings are not broadcasted. For instance, consider a female relative (we will call her Gwen) who is tasked with imparting traditional wisdom to brides. She teaches women various techniques to keep their marriages strong, placing the burden of ensuring the husband's fidelity on the woman. She further asserts that a man's infidelity should not be considered a big issue, as it is an expected behaviour from any man.

[8.] Bemba word refereeing to a traditional teacher. Can be male: shi - Chimbusa and female: na-Chimbusa

However, it is no secret that Gwen's own marriage is in shambles. Her husband has mistresses she is aware of, and he has even fathered children with one of them. The disillusionment and pain of maintaining the marriage weigh heavily on her, and it is clear she is breaking down under the strain. Her lessons clearly do not work, but she is still called upon as an example and teacher of perseverance and adherence to tradition, regardless of her personal circumstances (aka Shipikisha Club).[9] Accordingly, this is expected to make it easy to maintain the moral fabric of society. Sadly, it does not.

This paradox highlights the complexities and contradictions within societal norms and traditions. It underscores the need for a more nuanced understanding of the moral fabric that binds society, recognising both its strengths and its flaws.

Morality varies from society to society, is rooted in culture, and evolves over time. Each society determines what is acceptable or right, setting standards or expectations that enable people to live harmoniously together. For instance, as mentioned, society deems it acceptable for Gwen to stick to her marriage; it would be unacceptable for her to walk away. She is seen as a pillar of strength and endurance, reflecting the societal values that prioritise perseverance in marriage.

Maintaining and enhancing harmony in a society involves politeness, honourific behaviour, inclusivity, and acceptability. Social interaction is the means through which culture is born and sustained, ensuring harmony and fostering personal relationships (Tao, 2017). The common cultural practices (morals) defined by a particular society have their own reasons for existence. Some aim to keep individuals innocent, protect them, and maintain

---

[9] It is not a physical club but a term used to describe women who remain in marriages despite the abuse from the husband. Sticking to it (endurance/shipikisha) despite all odds. Leaving such a marriage is considered as a weakness and those who leave are a laughing stock in the community. Such women are not considered as teachers in society for fear of them misleading young potential wives.

order. Others, however, can be designed with 'ill' intent, to keep individuals bound to that particular culture.

Society often hides the truth behind some cultural practices. Gaining knowledge outside common cultural practices or questioning their purpose is not appreciated, and suggestions for change can be seen as a sign of a broken moral fibre. For example, a woman wearing a short dress or skirt was, and still is, not appreciated by the older generation. It is indicative of a broken moral fibre. In the 90s and 2000s, men and other women would sometimes publicly strip a woman naked for wearing a short dress, skirt, or tight trousers, as a warning and deterrent to others.

I recall an incident while travelling from the Copperbelt in 2007. I was seated next to an elderly lady. When we arrived at Kapiri Mposhi, a white lady boarded the bus. She was wearing white slacks and a short T-shirt that barely covered her navel. As she stretched to put her bag on the top rack, her T-shirt rose, almost exposing her bra. The elderly lady beside me began cursing and muttering, pointing at the white lady. She was visibly upset by what she perceived as inappropriate attire, reflecting her cultural values and the expectations of her generation.

These kinds of people are foolish, and morally destroy our children. Look at this dressing? Mmm?

At this point, she turned to face me.

"Look at her underwear showing, the navel with a ring. Her bra is almost visible. Mmm? Where do these people originate from? Do they even grow up with their mothers to guide and teach them sound values? Have you seen our children now? Our culture protected our children from such rubbish and now they are everywhere teaching our children their rubbish culture in the name of education. You hear that?"

She asked me. But before I could respond, she continued,

"Our children think copying this rubbish culture puts them at par with a white man and makes them look educated. Rubbish! Mmmssiiiiiii"

She ended by kissing her teeth, producing a loud sound that could have lasted more than a second. I hoped the poor white lady did not understand the Bemba language used, though I have no doubt she knew she was the one being talked about.

The elderly lady's outburst on the bus reflects deep-seated cultural beliefs and concerns about morality and cultural preservation. Her comments express frustration and disapproval towards what she perceives as inappropriate dressing and its influence on younger generations. Her remarks suggest a belief that such attire threatens traditional values and exposes children to what she views as damaging influences. Her questioning of the origins and upbringing of those who dress in a manner she disapproves of reflects a broader concern about cultural transmission and parental guidance. She laments the perceived erosion of cultural norms that she believes once protected children from what she describes as "rubbish culture." Her reference to "education" implies a perceived link between modern attire and aspirations to mimic Western standards, which she sees as detrimental rather than beneficial.

Further still, the elderly lady's use of strong language and gestures, including kissing her teeth, underscores her frustration and sense of cultural betrayal. While her remarks may seem harsh or intolerant to some, they illustrate a clash between traditional values and evolving cultural influences. This encounter highlights the complexities of cultural identity, generational differences, and the ongoing debate over the preservation versus adaptation of cultural practices in a changing world. This example illustrates how societal norms and expectations shape perceptions of morality and acceptable behaviour. While some cultural practices are designed to protect and maintain order, others may be rooted in outdated or harmful beliefs. It is important to recognise the dynamic nature of culture and morality and to be open to questioning and evolving these practices to better serve the needs and values of society.

The incident involving the First Lady of Nigeria commenting on fashion and moral fabric in comparison to Meghan Markle's visit illustrates a clash of cultural perspectives on attire and societal norms. This was noted by Emma Guinness of The Independent.[10]

According to Emma Guinness, the First Lady of Nigeria expressed concerns about what she perceived as a breakdown in the moral fabric, specifically citing Nigerian women adopting fashions that she felt were overly revealing or inappropriate. She quoted, "The message here is we have to salvage our children. We see the way they dress," referring film stars from America. Her remarks suggest a belief that certain styles of dress do not align with traditional Nigerian values and may contribute to what she sees as a decline in moral standards. The timing of her speech, following Meghan Markle's visit, suggests a possible link drawn between Western influences in fashion and perceptions of moral decline. Meghan Markle, known for her contemporary and sometimes daring fashion choices, may have unintentionally become a symbol in this discourse about cultural values and attire.

The First Lady's comments likely resonated with segments of Nigerian society that prioritise modesty and traditional values in dress. However, they also sparked debate about cultural authenticity, personal expression, and the influence of global fashion trends. Such discussions often reflect broader anxieties about cultural identity and the impact of globalisation on local traditions.

Overall, this example highlights how discussions about fashion can intersect with larger societal debates about morality, cultural preservation, and the perceived influence of foreign cultures. It

---

[10] Emma Guinness (2024). Nigeria's First Lady slams US celebs just days after Meghan Markle visit: 'We don't accept nakedness' 9CommentsNigeria's First Lady slams US celebs just days after Meghan Markle visit: 'We don't accept nakedness' | The Independent

underscores the complexity of navigating cultural change while preserving cultural identity and values in a globalised world.

For a long time, our cultural beliefs have often attributed blame to Western culture for what is perceived as the decay of our moral fabric. The shifting cultural norms influenced by Western lifestyles are frequently linked to this perception of a broken moral fabric. While some aspects may indeed contribute to societal challenges, it would be simplistic and unfair to place all the blame on Western culture alone.

Central to our moral fabric is a golden thread woven from our own culture and traditions, referred to in the Bemba dialect as "intambi." These intambi provide us with a profound sense of identity and belonging. Older generations often use the phrase "te intambi shesu" to denote something they believe to be influenced by the West. It's important to recognise that culture is dynamic and constantly evolving. While external influences can impact cultural practices, our intambi remain foundational to our values and societal cohesion. They serve as a repository of wisdom, guiding principles, and norms that have sustained us through generations.

Rather than solely blaming external influences, it is crucial to engage in nuanced discussions about cultural change and adaptation. This includes evaluating which aspects of change enhance our society and which may challenge our values. By embracing our intambi while also acknowledging the complexities of cultural exchange, we can navigate these challenges with respect for both tradition and progress.

The Culture of Silence

In Zambia, sex remains a taboo subject, an awkward elephant in the room that everyone acknowledges but pretends doesn't exist. The expectation is that younger individuals and those unmarried should be entirely unaware of it. When a child brings up questions about sex, they are quickly silenced, being told it's bad manners to discuss such topics. This societal silence surrounding sex, in all its forms—consensual, non-consensual, or dubious consent—is seen as a way to preserve the innocence of the young at all costs.

As a result, we often blame the West, social media, and modernisation for the erosion of our moral fabric, while ignoring our own role in perpetuating harm by burying our heads in the sand.

Additionally, our society does not condone parents teaching their own children anything sexual. Hence, at pubescent or before marriage, this role is traditionally assigned to the "nacimbusa/shicimbusa." Grandparents and sometimes aunties are allowed to provide this education. The total dependence on an external figure to teach such a delicate but serious topic is often underestimated. Furthermore, society expects older siblings or extended family members to begin to teach the topic. There seems to be a tendency to assume that the young will only discover sex when they come of age. This, inadvertently, does more harm than good.

Sexual assault and violence are not new phenomena in our societies or culture. The tendency to conceal these acts and the monsters is a major reason for their continued perpetuation, rather than being significantly influenced by Western culture. By treating sex as an unspoken taboo, we create an environment where sexual assault and violence can thrive unchecked and unchallenged.

Our cultural fabric is complex, interwoven with threads whose real meanings are often obscured. While there are undeniable problems and decay within this tapestry, the outward appearance remains beautiful, foundational, and something to be preserved at all costs. This dynamic is exemplified by our culture's emphasis on respect for elders, especially men, without exception. In Zambia, respect is deeply ingrained and often demanded, especially from women and younger individuals towards men. This respect is not inherently negative; for instance, individuals are given the prefix

'Ba' upon reaching puberty, as in 'Ba John' or 'Ba Jane,' a term of respect. Others, depending on their age, are given titles such as uncle, aunty, mummy, daddy, or grandparent, even if they are not members of the family. This is a form of respect. However, while every adult is expected to be respected, the respect accorded to men is particularly emphasised and often demanded.

This male superiority over women is seen as crucial, regardless of age. Such cultural practices, while seemingly benign or even positive at a glance, can contribute to an environment where abuses of power are overlooked and unaddressed. When respect is demanded without exception, it can silence victims and protect perpetrators, especially in cases of sexual violence. By refusing to discuss sex openly and honestly, and by maintaining rigid hierarchies of respect, we create a fertile ground for abuse to continue under the guise of preserving cultural values. It should be understood that there is nothing wrong with according respect to elderly people, nor does this book advocate for the removal of respect. Rather, this book is concerned with the tendency to prioritise respect over addressing and dealing with the perpetrator, who in most cases is older than the victim.

Therefore, a critical aspect of addressing sexual violence and improving our cultural fabric involves challenging these harmful practices. We must strike a balance between preserving the valuable aspects of our cultural heritage and adapting to changing times. This means being willing to openly discuss difficult topics like sex and recognising that silence and repression can do more harm than good. We need to create an environment where individuals feel safe to speak out against abuse and where respect is earned and reciprocal, rather than demanded based on gender or age. Only then can we create a society that is truly harmonious and just.

The Bemba saying, "Umwaume tachepa",[11] meaning any male, irrespective of their age, has the potential to make a woman

---

[11.] A Bemba proverb: 'a man is never too small'

pregnant or is seen as a maker of serious decisions—illustrates a deeply rooted cultural belief. At a glance, this respect may seem benign or even positive. However, it can also foster an environment where vices such as sexual harassment are culturally protected and even perpetuated. The respect demanded of men can create an environment where women and children feel unable to speak out against abuse. It can become a tool for silencing victims and shielding abusers. This is compounded by the fact that these abuses often occur in places that should be safe for the victim, such as homes, schools, offices, and churches. Perpetrators can be family members, friends, teachers, peers, pastors, church mates, workmates, and neighbours.

It is no secret that Zambia faces high rates of defilement, molestation, and rape. While some incidents are committed by strangers, the majority involve perpetrators who are known to the victims. Research from various sources, including WHO (2020), McQuade (2014), and Adefolalu (2014), supports this observation. Furthermore, the Darkness to Light (2015) report argues that perpetrators, especially those who molest children, often look and act like everyone else. They tend to be innocent-looking, making it harder to identify and more difficult to report. There is a need to ensure:

Education and Awareness

1. Sex Education: Implement comprehensive sex education in schools that includes discussions about consent, respect, and the importance of reporting abuse.

2. Community Programmes: Develop community-based programmes to raise awareness about the importance of speaking out against sexual abuse and violence.

Legal and Policy Changes

1. Strengthening Laws: Strengthen and enforce laws against sexual violence and harassment, ensuring that perpetrators

are held accountable regardless of their social status or position.

2. Support Systems: Establish robust support systems for victims, including counselling services, safe houses, and legal assistance.

Cultural Shifts

1. Challenging Norms: Encourage open discussions that challenge harmful cultural norms and promote gender equality.

2. Role Models: Highlight positive role models who advocate for respect, equality, and the protection of all individuals, regardless of gender or age.

Community Involvement

1. Grassroots Movements: Support grassroots movements that work to change cultural perceptions and protect victims of sexual violence.

2. Inclusivity in Decision-Making: Ensure that women and young people are included in decision-making processes at all levels of society.

By addressing these cultural and societal issues head-on, Zambia can create a more just and safer environment for all its citizens. Respect should be mutual and earned, not demanded based on outdated cultural norms. Creating a society where everyone feels safe and respected requires both cultural and systemic changes.

Ennis's Story

I was almost raped when I was 14 years old by a teacher who called me to his office to be disciplined for an offence I did not even understand. However, he was the adult and so I didn't question him when summoned to his office. I turned up in obedience. Once I was in his office, he locked the door behind him and before I knew what was happening, he was pinning me down on the floor. I went into survival mode. I kicked every which way for my dear life. In the process, I accidentally kicked his dear 'tools' (manhood) rendering them useless for the job. He let go of me to attend to them in pain. I got up, quickly rushed to the door, unlocked it and ran to class without looking back. My desk mate had told my teacher that I had gone for punishment, therefore, I was not questioned when I got in. I was panting and shaking. The female teacher never questioned my deportment or my roughed-up state as my uniform was covered in dust and my hair was everywhere. That was not me at all. My desk mate looked shocked but I was so afraid to say anything. I never told anyone. It was my secret.

When sexual violence and assault occur within the nuclear or extended family, the taboo nature of the issue often leads to its cover-up. Society has long conditioned us to view sexual predators as inhumane, strange monsters, making it difficult to reconcile the fact that a family member could commit such acts. Consequently, the vice is often handled privately, with the hope that it was a one-time occurrence that won't happen again. In these cases, the truth becomes relative—upheld only if it does not cause inconvenience to the family. Common responses include:

➤ "You can't report him; he is your brother!"

➤ "You will destroy your mother; you will break her heart if she finds out this has happened."

➤ "You know you are not supposed to talk about that!"

➤ "You must learn to forgive and move on; that's still your father/uncle/brother."

➤ "What has happened, has happened; let it go, family is all that matters."

Protecting and maintaining family ties often take precedence over addressing the wrongdoing. Children are consistently and insistently taught to respect without question. For example, a female child may be expected to put on a chitenge [12] when around "Uncle X," without being given the reasons why. Instead of addressing the real issue by telling "Uncle X" to stop visiting to protect the girl, the responsibility is unfairly placed on the child. Children should be warned to be cautious around certain family members, like "Uncle X," regardless of his relationship to the parents, whether he is "mum's elder brother" or "daddy's younger brother." Below is a story told by a Tamuzu.

Tamuzu's Story

I live in a two-roomed house, one bedroom and a sitting room. My 12-year-old daughter sleeps in the sitting room. My husband goes drinking every day and returns home in the early hours. One night, past midnight, he arrives home with a drunken friend and declares that he will sleep in the sitting room with our 14-year-old daughter. Imagine! This man is completely drunk. How do we risk our daughter with him? My husband sees nothing wrong and starts a fight to get me to give in. I walked into the sitting room, took my daughter and walked out at that hour to my brother's house which was almost 45 minutes away at that hour. No one supported my decision. I was condemned by everyone who wanted to know why I had gone to my brother's house that late. Everyone is saying, "he wouldn't have done anything, he is her father's friend and so, just as good as her father; what was wrong with him sharing the room with the girl; isn't that being disrespectful of your husband; you are just being paranoid; if you cannot trust your husband's friend, who will you trust?" I don't care what they are saying, no one will damage my child, she narrated.

The majority of those who condemned this lady were fellow women. The problem with this method of dealing with the vice is that the assaulted person is forced to live with the fact

---

[12.] A 2 meters wrapper that women wrap around their waist.

that something happened to them while maintaining a forced or pretend harmonious unity. The victim goes through life thinking that what happened was somehow their fault or that nothing wrong occurred. Meanwhile, the assaulter is protected and learns that his actions bear no responsibility or consequences. This lack of accountability can turn what might have been an isolated incident into a recurring habit. Family silence thus contributes significantly to violence and assault being normalised.

Sexual Beings

In some cultures, as noted by WHO (2020), sexual intercourse is considered a man's right or a sign of masculinity. This is true of our culture. Despite treating sex as a taboo issue, it seems to permit or give a pass to men and boys. This perception frames sex as a component of masculinity. Consequently, when sexual violence or assault occurs, it is often dismissed with phrases like "boys being boys" or "that's the nature of men." Men and boys are seen and accepted as sexual beings, and their actions are excused on this basis. As a result, women and girls are considered responsible for keeping men's sexual urges at bay. Hence, demands of dressing modestly. The lack of community and legal sanctions against identified or known perpetrators exacerbates the vice in question.

The vice is neatly and tightly hidden within the cultural fabric, so much so that any attempt to expose it is met with reactions such as:

1. "He did not mean to hurt you."
2. "Do not tell anyone because he can go to prison for what was just a mistake."
3. "He will not repeat it."
4. "He is my brother's son. Don't worry, the family will talk to him about it, and he will never do this again."

5. "Are you sure? This is my brother you are talking about, and he has never done this before."

6. "That is why I say, always wear a chitenge around your uncle. You see now. Make sure you wear a chitenge around him from now on."

7. "You are even lucky it is a relative. Take more care; next time it could be a stranger."

8. "What were you doing in his room?" "What was he doing in your room?"

9. "Why did you not lock the door to the bedroom/bathroom?"

10. "Don't worry, you can go and live with your grandmother so he does not do this again."

11. "These things happen, but keep it a secret. This remains in the family. Tell no one, please. The next time it happens, tell me."

12. "You can't tell anyone what happened. He is the one supporting us."

13. "Your mother's husband did this? Do not tell your mother. She will lose her marriage, and you will all be left with nowhere to go."

These reactions are indicative of a broken moral fabric. They attempt to mend a decaying cultural tapestry by suppressing the truth and protecting the perpetrator. The concept of dirty secrets is premised on the expectation, decision, or 'willingness' to keep an act secret to protect the perpetrator. The victim is under immense pressure to keep the secret for the sake of maintaining the family's image, relationship, job, or status quo. The perpetrator remains protected and, in some cases, continues to violate the victim while enjoying impunity.

The Parental Role

A common Zambian adage states, "A child is only yours when in the womb; once born, it belongs to the rest of the community."

This reflects the cultural norm where the community shares the responsibility of disciplining and caring for any child as needed. This practice remains prevalent in rural areas, where any adult can discipline a misbehaving child. The community's moral expectations demand collective responsibility to ensure children grow up within cultural confines.

Parents face boundaries regarding how far they can go in teaching their children, especially on sensitive topics like sex. As already indicated, it is considered taboo and immoral for parents to discuss sex directly with their children. As a result, children's questions about sex are often unanswered, diverted, or delegated to grandparents, uncles, and aunts. In the absence of such relatives, well-known community members or appointed traditional teachers handle this responsibility. While modern families may see some changes, this practice persists.

The division of responsibilities in teaching children is also clear. Female children are traditionally taught by their aunts, grandmothers, and other women, while boys are taught by their fathers and male relatives. It is not a collective duty of both parents. If a girl becomes pregnant out of wedlock, she is labelled challenging, headstrong, or promiscuous, and the mother is blamed for failing to discipline her properly. Conversely, if a boy impregnates a girl, engages in promiscuous behaviour, or becomes a public nuisance, the father is not blamed. Instead, the behaviour is excused with sayings like "boys will be boys" or "he just needs to grow up and mature".

Despite these provisions, communication channels, especially regarding sex and its associated risks, are rarely open or encouraged. This lack of open dialogue leads to many victims remaining silent and perpetrators escaping responsibility. Consequently, harmful behaviours are perpetuated, and cultural practices continue to shield wrongdoers while failing to protect the vulnerable.

Collectivism

The extended family plays a crucial role in Zambian culture, reinforcing the collective theory that underpins social interactions. Any relative, regardless of how distant, is important and should be welcomed and made to feel at home, irrespective of the available space in the house. However, some "extended family" connections are ambiguous and difficult to trace. These connections often stem from people coming from the same village or area, leading to bonds that create familial ties. Additionally, friendships forged by parents can lead to children growing up knowing their parents' friends as uncles and aunts, and their children as cousins or close family friends.

While this practice is admirable and indicative of a strong moral fabric, it can also pose risks. Little is known about some of these individuals' backgrounds, yet they are readily welcomed and given unprecedented access to families. For instance, a father might call and say his friend is stranded in your area and needs a place to stay. Out of respect and obligation, the child will open their home, viewing the friend as an uncle. Subsequently, each time this "uncle" is in town, he feels free to visit and stay.

These family members often feel entitled to visit and tend to stay as long as they want. They also feel entitled to ask for support, and in most cases, this support is provided. This practice underscores the value placed on family ties and collective responsibility but also highlights the potential vulnerabilities within the cultural framework.

The open-door policy towards extended family and quasi-relatives reflects a commitment to community and mutual support. However, it also necessitates a balance between maintaining cultural traditions and ensuring the safety and well-being of family members, especially the younger and more vulnerable ones.

Amai's Story

When I was young, a 'distant' relative of my father visited us. I was 10 years old. He apparently had been in prison for some years. My father welcomed him to our house so that he could help him find a job. We were warned never to tell anyone about his prison status. His importance to the family was clearly explained, and he deserved respect as good as that which we gave our parents. He lived with us for months. He hardly went out of the house as he did not want to be known by any outsiders. He began calling me "my little wife". As a child, I did not understand the endearing title, but I loved it. I giggled and laughed each time he called me "my little wife". I was comfortable with him, and I could go to his bedroom anytime. One day, mum left me in charge of his breakfast because she was going to the market early in the morning. She left it already made on the tray. I was supposed to take it to his bedroom when he was up. Somehow, my brothers left the house to play, and I was all alone with him.

I heard sounds in his bedroom and hence knocked on his door asking if I could bring in his breakfast. He said yes. He opened the door and I brought his breakfast. "My little wife is at it," he said as I put the tray on the small table beside his bed. As I turned to leave, he stopped me and said, "now my little wife, where are you going without playing your wifely duties." Not knowing what he was up to, I turned back giggling. 'Lay on the bed," he said and I did as asked, lying on my side. "No, you lie on your back," he said smiling. So, I did that. To my surprise, he got on top of me. I screamed, pushing him away with my small hands and legs. "You are heavy," I said, crying. I was not able to breathe because of his weight on top of me. "It won't take long," he said as he tried to pull my underwear down. I screamed my lungs out. He then jumped off me, and I ran out of the bedroom. Five minutes later, he came looking for me. I was still confused at what had just happened; in my mind, I thought what had happened was him wanting to kill me. I hadn't the faintest idea this was attempted rape. "My little wife, don't tell anyone what happened. I just wanted to check if my wife was ready for her duties. Your mum will beat you if you tell her any of this, you hear that?" I nodded my head in agreement, wiping off my tears. He wasn't wrong; my mother was well known for dishing out beatings, and so, I kept that secret. My mother never learned about this ordeal.

Many can analyse this experience and provide their perspectives. In a victim-blaming society, some might judge and say a girl of 10 should have known better or that a mother should never have left a girl child alone with a man. While some of this reasoning might be well-intentioned, the critical issue remains: who committed the offence? Did he seize an unexpected opportunity, or had he meticulously planned his actions? The "my little wife" endearment, which meant nothing in the innocent world of the girl, cannot justify his attempted abuse. The bottom line is that what he exposed the young girl to was unequivocally wrong. It is important to note that the perpetrator is the master planner. They do not just pounce on the victim suddenly; the whole situation is carefully planned. The victim merely falls into the skillful trap, yet the blame often falls on the victim.

Amai was innocent and had not even reached puberty. She was comfortable and trusted him, after all, he was brought into the home by the parents. Our cultural traditions often allow for such endearing terms. Older men might call young girls "wife," just as older women might call young boys "husband." Cousins may refer to each other as wife and husband, and grandparents might use similar terms of endearment for their grandchildren. These are just a few examples, which vary across cultures. There is nothing inherently wrong with such endearments when they remain just that. However, abuse can occur under the guise of these relationships. For some, these terms are used to groom or create an environment of trust between the child and the adult.

Families, both nuclear and extended, often protect each other to the extent that devastating secrets are kept silent to prevent family destruction and maintain their status quo in society. For instance, when a "distant" relative with a dubious family connection crosses the line, the family may not readily speak out due to the potential ridicule this could bring upon them. This silence is pervasive and damaging. It perpetuates a cycle where the perpetrator is shielded, and the victim is left to deal with the trauma in isolation. The family's reputation is often prioritised over the well-being of the individual. This cultural inclination to protect family honour at all costs results in a lack of accountability for the perpetrator and a lack of justice for the victim.

Culture is a foundational aspect of individual identity, serving as the bedrock of who we are. However, culture is dynamic and should be allowed to evolve with time. Who we are will inevitably change as certain cultural practices become obsolete or lose their original purpose.

For example, our forefathers had specific reasons for keeping a fire burning in the house:

1. To ward off the spirits of the dead, believed to hover around the living and pose dangers.
2. To provide support and counsel to mourners.
3. To keep dangerous animals away.

The same applies to keeping a fire going in the house the whole night:

1. To provide light and warmth on cold nights.
2. To deter mosquitoes with the smoke.
3. To preserve the fire for the next day's use.

Our environment has changed significantly since then. Housing styles have evolved, and we no longer live in areas surrounded by dangerous wildlife. Modern lighting and heating systems have replaced the need for fire to provide light and warmth. Additionally, fire can now be made using various sources. These changes render the traditional practice of hundreds of people sleeping at a funeral house unnecessary.

While providing support and counsel to mourners (points 1 and 2) remains crucial, it does not require hundreds of supporters spending the night at the funeral house. This tradition persists largely for its own sake, often placing a significant financial burden on the family of the deceased to feed the mourners.

Cultural practices should be flexible enough to adapt to contemporary realities, ensuring they remain relevant and supportive of the community's current needs. There could be other reasons beyond those mentioned, but they are no longer valuable. We can no longer claim the necessity of keeping a fire burning in the house. Even if it was an important practice then, it is not now. The people and the environment are no longer the same. Other instances include the following:

1. It is no longer necessary to expect men to hunt animals for food because butcheries are now widespread. Even in villages, there are restrictions due to factors such as protecting endangered species and preserving wildlife.

2. Women are no longer expected to pound maize meal or cassava meal because there are millers to do the job, relieving women of this backbreaking task. Women may not even have the time to undertake such tasks.

3. The expectations around marriage age have changed. Previously, culture required a girl of pubescent age to get married right after reaching puberty as there was no formal schooling. Now, every girl and boy has the right to an education.

4. It is no longer necessary to withdraw a girl from school for 2 to 3 months to initiate her into womanhood and then marry her after the ceremony. While society once considered this initiation practice crucial, it is no longer important. However, some cultures have modified the initiation to accommodate contemporary values.

Education has informed us with better thinking skills that enable us to assess what is relevant and what is not. It allows us to question the relevance of practices that were intended to keep us from such privileges. Society is now better informed about other cultures too. It is important to develop strategies to maintain relevant and useful cultural practices so that what defines us is not lost.

We must teach our children how to remain loyal to their roots and value their culture, ensuring that the baby is kept after throwing out the bathwater. Keeping redundant practices under the guise of maintaining our moral fabric can contribute to its decay. It is not solely Western influence that causes this decay. When people refuse to change with the times or fail to modify damaging practices, a rot, like in nature, begins to occur and spread.

Below is an old parable or allegory that has been shared a number of times to demonstrate a dated practice.

One day after school, a young girl noticed that her mom was cutting off the ends of a pot roast before putting it in the oven to cook for dinner. She had seen her mom do this many times before but had never asked her why. So, this time she asked, and her mom replied, "I don't know why I cut the ends off, but it's what my mom always did. Why don't you ask your Grandma?" So the young girl called her grandmother on the phone and said, "Grandma, why do you cut the ends off the pot roast before cooking it?" Her grandmother replied, "I don't know. That's just the way my mom always cooked it. Why don't you ask her?" Undeterred, the girl called her great-grandmother, who was living in a nursing home, and asked her the same question. "Why did you cut the ends off the pot roast before cooking it?"

And her great-grandmother did not reply, "I cut off the ends of the pot roast because that's what my mother did." She did not say it makes the meat juicier. She said, "When I was first married, we had a very small oven, and the pot roast didn't fit in the oven unless I cut the ends off." Narrated by Kibbe Madora (2014).

The question is: why did the mother of this girl, and probably many others, continue cutting off the ends of the roast when their ovens are much larger than the small oven her great-grandmother had? The practice was relevant then, but times had changed. The young girl's questioning of this tradition highlights its current irrelevance. She recognised the waste of the roast, the waste of time and energy, and the practice's stifling effect on their ability to think critically, leading them to follow tradition blindly despite having a larger oven. Insisting on this practice is pointless, as there is no longer a need for it.

Knowledge is good and important. It's essential to remember where we have come from and the paths those before us walked. However, those paths are long gone. We can learn from them to avoid certain pitfalls, but holding on to them despite the damage they cause is folly and a disservice to future generations. Knowledge is not permanent; it may be useful only up to a certain point, after which it should be reviewed, discarded, or upgraded. It changes and can be improved upon.

We know we have a problem with sexual violence and assault, so it's time to speak up. Sex is not going away, and pretending it does not exist is foolish. Not speaking about it and keeping it a taboo has clearly not worked in our favour. We need to continue to speak out against sexual vices, not wait until we are older to tell our stories, and not silence or shame those who do speak up. It's time to create safe spaces for victims as well as perpetrators to heal. We must face the reality that the tapestry we are guarding at such a high cost is not worth the price of another generation. The moral fabric has been decaying and, in some areas, is completely decayed. It's time to change the threads, to create a better tapestry that others will build on and be proud of.

06

SHE

From the moment the words "It's a girl!" are spoken, after the initial joy comes a thick lump in a mother's throat—one she can't quite shake. The thought that one day, this innocent being may endure the same pain she herself has known is hard to bear.

Yet, the pride in a mother's heart remains unspoken.

"If I have endured it, so will she," the mother thinks. "It is her lot, and she will survive it."

The unbearable comes when abuse taints the rhythm of her daughter's life. What should define her identity becomes a trophy for another.

Something too desirable to devour rather than to explore with care and reverence.

The pleasure meant for the rightful seeker is stolen without authority.

Her innocence skips freely around the house, yet her heart is weighed down with pain and remorse.

Shhhhhh! The devourer waits just outside the door, and the keys in her small hands seem powerless to lock away the treasure within.

07

Misconceptions

The image and role of women have been, and continue to be, distorted in many cultures. Women are not second-class human beings; they are as human as men, differing only in biological makeup. For example, a tree is a tree regardless of its structure. Some trees produce fruit, others do not. While some are constantly in bloom with beautiful flowers, others are seasonal, blossoming only in certain environments or seasons. Still, others never produce flowers or fruit, providing only shade and a habitat for various animals and insects. The fact remains: they are all trees. None is superior to the other. Simply because one tree is good for charcoal does not make it superior to the tree that just provides a home to many insects.

The same is true for human beings. One is female, while the other is male. One has larger, fuller breasts, a womb to incubate a baby, and the capability to give birth, while the other can only provide the seed (sperm), but does not have milk-producing breasts. This difference does not mean the one with the capacity to receive sperm, incubate life, and give birth is inferior. Neither is the one who provides the sperm superior, as his sperm is useless without the other. The makeup and functionality may differ, but the fact remains: we are all human. Our differences should be celebrated, not used as a source of debates and arguments.

This chapter will explore various misconceptions that have been created about women and how these misconceptions have influenced the treatment, behaviour, and societal expectations about women. Many of these misconceptions are deeply entrenched in our culture. Unfortunately, the majority of the culprits perpetuating and safeguarding these misconceptions are women themselves.

The Religious Misconception

Zambia is a declared Christian nation, though it hosts various other religions as well. This section focuses on the Christian standpoint and the misconceptions that have emerged therein.

The Bible provides a law, or rather a blueprint, for the family, establishing that for the sake of order in the home, God placed leadership in the man, making him "the head" of **his home**. Many interpret this to mean that men, by virtue of being male, are leaders in every sphere of life. They argue that a man needs respect and obedience at all costs because his leadership role is divinely appointed. It is important to note that Jesus, was also divinely appointed as head of the church, and he serves the very people he leads.

The expectation for men to be dominant and women to be submissive has unfortunately led to the subjugation and abuse of women. This issue is not unique to Zambia or Africa; it is a universal problem and remains a contentious subject. Even people who claim to be agnostic often uphold this view.

Sir John Dalberg-Acton, 8th Baronet, made a timeless remark: "Power tends to corrupt, and absolute power corrupts absolutely." This is evident in many parts of Zambia. When a man is given absolute or somewhat unchallenged power simply because he is genetically male, it can create monsters who fail to take responsibility for their actions or be held accountable. While acknowledging that men hold headship in their homes, it is crucial to understand the true meaning and application of leadership. An abusive leader in any organisation is a tyrant or, in some cases, a dictator. Rarely does anything good come from this type of leadership, and the same can be said for the home.

Men were not given the role of leader to dominate or subjugate women. They were given leadership to bring about order, to provide guidance in marriage (the keyword being "marriage"), and to serve, not to be served. Women too are supposed to be submissive to their husbands in their homes, not to every male. Nowhere in the Bible is it written that by making men the heads of households, women were relegated to an inferior position.

However, the theory advanced by fact and implication is that women are inferior and below men. This misconception is reflected not only in marriage but in almost every sphere of life, perpetuating numerous other misconceptions about women. Culture has further entrenched this inferiority of women, hinging it on a biblical misconception of man. The leadership position accorded to men in marriage has been misconstrued as a sign of superiority over all women. The masculine physique of men has also been mistakenly seen as an image of superiority, as has their reproductive role. God never said that.

Understanding and correcting these misconceptions is essential for fostering a society where both men and women are valued equally, each contributing uniquely to the community and the family.

Male and female are created in the image of God, equally endowed with dominion over all things. Genesis presents an equality of the genders, not male dominance or leadership. In Genesis 2:18-19, woman is created as a corresponding partner to man. The text describes woman as being created to be the man's 'ezer kenegdo,' which, when translated literally, means 'a strength corresponding to him.' Unfortunately, the word 'ezer' is often translated to mean 'helper' in English. However, 'ezer' in the Bible does not suggest a helper in terms of a 'servant.' The term 'ezer' appears multiple times in the Old Testament, often referring to God as a helper to humans, indicating a role of strength and support rather than subservience. For instance, in Psalms, God is frequently referred to as our 'help' or 'helper'

(Psalm 33:20, 70:5, 115:9-11). Clearly, this context suggests strength and partnership rather than inferiority.

The misconception that 'ezer' implies a subordinate role has contributed to a distorted view of gender roles within Christianity. The idea that women are created to be mere helpers, secondary to men, is a misinterpretation that undermines the biblical portrayal of equality and mutual support. In reality, Genesis 1:27 emphasises that both men and women are created in God's image: "So God created mankind in his own image, in the image of God he created them; male and female he created them." This verse underscores the fundamental equality of men and women in their creation and purpose. Absolutely, sameness does not equate to equality. It is undeniable that men and women are different, both biologically and in various other aspects. These differences are fundamental and contribute to the richness and diversity of human experience.

Biologically, men and women have distinct physical characteristics, hormonal profiles, and reproductive roles. These differences are evident in anatomy, physiology, and genetic makeup. Beyond biology, men and women often have different perspectives, experiences, and approaches to life based on societal roles, cultural influences, and personal backgrounds.

Recognising and celebrating these differences does not imply inequality. Equality between men and women means acknowledging and respecting these differences while ensuring that both genders have equal rights, opportunities, and access to resources. It means valuing each individual for their unique contributions and abilities, rather than adhering to rigid stereotypes or roles based on gender.

Correcting these misconceptions is crucial for fostering a more accurate understanding of biblical teachings on gender. By recognising the equal value and complementary strengths of both men and women, we can move towards a more just and harmonious interpretation of scripture that aligns with the original intent of equality and partnership, not sameness. We shall never be the same. We were created with differences (biological) but we are both equal human beings.

Arguably the most authoritative biblical Hebrew dictionary lists the biblical meanings of 'ezer' as "help, assistance, might, and strength," but not "helper." This distinction is significant as it emphasises the role of the woman as an equal partner endowed with strength and support rather than a subordinate."[13] Women are man's counterparts; they were never created to be subordinate to men. The misconception of women's inferiority does not hold much water in reality, despite its persistent grip that continues to harm women. While physical differences exist, this is not the debate. Women's bodies and physiques are different from men's, but this difference does not imply inferiority.

Women have cared for homes, raised children, and at times, even taken care of husbands who never matured but merely grew older. Women endure the intense physical ordeal of labour, risking their lives for another, and yet, the world continues to witness daily, even hourly, births. Women navigate through the pain of pre- and post-menstruation while still managing their responsibilities at home, in business, or at work. This endurance and resilience highlight that women are not inferior in mentality or spirituality to their male counterparts. Otherwise, the monthly pain and the agony of childbirth would mentally destroy them.

It is crucial to emphasise that we are discussing equality, not identicalness. Gloria Steinem aptly stated that "the human race is like a bird with 2 wings; if one is broken, the bird can't fly." For the bird to soar, both wings must equally pull their weight. Men and women are like the wings of a bird. A bird with one wing cannot fly, and one wing cannot be considered superior merely because it is on the right side. If one wing assumes authority

---

[13]. Ludwig Koehler, Walter Baumgartner, and Johann Jakob Stamm, Hebrew and Aramaic Lexicon of the Old Testament, 5 vols. (Leiden:Bill 1994-200), 2 (1995): 811-812

over the other, the entire bird is compromised. As a society, we must realise that to reach the highest heights, both wings must be equal.

In the context of equality, diversity is not a barrier but a strength. Embracing diversity allows societies to benefit from the full spectrum of human potential and creativity. It encourages collaboration, understanding, and innovation across different perspectives and experiences. Therefore, while men and women are indeed different, equality requires ensuring that these differences do not result in discrimination, oppression, or unequal treatment. It entails promoting fairness, justice, and equal dignity for all individuals, regardless of gender or any other characteristic.

Let us make human beings in our image, in our likeness, so that they may rule over the fish in the sea and the birds in the sky, over the livestock and all the wild animals, and over all the creatures that move along the ground. So, God created human beings in his own image, in the image of God he created them; **MALE AND FEMALE, HE CREATED THEM.**[14][15]

Male and female were created in his image and in his own likeness. It is clear enough for anyone to conclude that God is both male and female, and this had to be demonstrated in the creation of the 2 genders. So, no one is better than the other as all are creations in God's own image and likeness.

In Galatians, we are told that "There is neither Jew nor Gentile, neither slave nor free, nor is there male and female, for you are all one in Christ Jesus."[16]

---

[14] Emphasis of capital letters and bolded by authors.

[15] Genesis 1:26 NIV

[16] Galatians 3:28 NIV

Dress Code

Dressing has undergone numerous changes over time. Live long enough, and you'll see fashion trends come full circle. Every generation seems to have its own dress code, which evolves or adapts the previous trends. Dress codes are influenced by the culture of the people, and since culture is dynamic, so is fashion. Additionally, global trends have a significant impact on dress codes. The theory of "umwana ashenda" (a child who does not travel, does not learn) no longer holds water because information about global trends is readily available at the click of a button. One need not travel to know what is happening elsewhere.

In most cultures in Zambia, the chitenge is a staple for women. While some families may not strictly require a woman or girl to wear a chitenge, it is widely accepted and often encouraged. In some families, girls are introduced to the chitenge as early as 6 years old so that they grow up appreciating this traditional wrapper. When a young woman meets her future in-laws for the first time, wearing a chitenge is seen as the best choice and makes a great first impression. Funerals are another occasion where a chitenge is a must-have.

However, the chitenge did not originate in Zambia. It traces its origins to Indonesia. You might wonder how it became such a significant part of our culture. Genuine Indonesian batik was very labour-intensive, beautiful, and expensive to produce. As European mills began automating the dyeing process to make the fabric more affordable, they saw an opportunity. There was competition between the British, French, and Dutch to mass-produce this seemingly profitable fabric. Vlisco, a Dutch company that started in 1846, emerged victorious in this competition, dominating the market and establishing itself so well that it is still in operation today. Vlisco began with genuine batiks and later moved on to reproductions of wax-printed batiks. This mass production made the chitenge more accessible and affordable, solidifying its place in Zambian culture.

While the chitenge is now an integral part of Zambian cultural attire, its origins remind us of the interconnectedness of global cultures and the dynamic nature of fashion. As trends continue to evolve, they reflect both our cultural heritage and our adaptability to global influences.

The idea was to mass-produce this cotton fabric, often wax-printed, and send it back to Indonesia. However, opportunities arose to sell it to Africans along the oceanic trading route to Indonesia. Over the years, patterns and colour palettes were adapted to West and Central African tastes. By the 1930s, Vlisco's fabrics were being designed specifically for the African elite. The business boomed, spreading across Africa, and by the 1950s, Vlisco was producing designs at the request of African traders. The fabric became commonly known as "wax hollandais."

As Zambia was birthed in the 1960s, the use of this fabric was already deeply entrenched. Though it was never originally ours, it became a traditional and cultural piece of cloth that embodied our identity as Africans. Zambia even set up a clothing factory and began producing our own designs, exporting it to neighbouring countries. In parts of Zimbabwe, the chitenge is referred to as "(a) Zambia."

The chitenge was and continues to be deeply rooted in our society, appearing at all important functions in our lives and serving various purposes:

1. **Propriety**: Women wore and wear the cloth as a presentable dress, suitable for work and significant occasions such as weddings.

2. **Uniform**: It is an acceptable outfit for specific occasions like funerals and traditional events (e.g., Chilanga Mulilos).

3. **Utility**: It is used for beddings, nappies, baby-carrying, and carrying heavy loads. Hospitals even request that a pregnant woman include a chitenge in her hospital bag.

4. **Identity**: It signifies African and Zambian identity, especially on Independence Day when the Zambian coat of arms, flag, and national colours are celebrated through the fabric, now produced in China.

The chitenge's history often leaves young African men and women, especially those without a national or traditional outfit, feeling confused about their cultural identity. It has become a fashion statement and is often considered Zambia's traditional wear, assuming a central role at most traditional events.

A crucial consideration is the chitenge's use as a wrapper that provides assumed decency in a woman's dressing. While this is understandable, it's important to note that no dress code should be used as a justification for sexually violating a female. This issue will be discussed extensively later in the book.

As previously discussed, culture is a powerful tool that informs people of who they are and how to behave. While culture encompasses many positive aspects, some negative facets can be particularly degrading and retrogressive, especially for women. Traditions serve as the medium through which culture is transmitted, facilitating the preservation of cultural norms.

Christian Religion and Dressing

In many societies, the Christian religion has been used to enforce dress codes and other behaviours, often targeting women. Some women, emerging as God's representatives, take it upon themselves to correct the dress code of other women, often using cultural norms as their justification.

The church, intended to be a place of sanctuary and moral guidance, has unfortunately become a venue where dirty secrets are kept. There have been numerous instances where pastors, elders, leaders, and priests have violated women, men, and boys, and these violations have been kept secret. When victims attempt to speak out, they are often not believed and are subjected to further psychological and social abuse.

A typical example can involve a woman being violated by a church leader. The narrative is often manipulated to portray the leader as an untouchable figure, while the woman is labelled as a Jezebel[17] or an agent of Satan sent to cause the downfall of an otherwise innocent "man of God." This pattern is not unique to any one denomination and is seen across various church congregations.

The church, whether intentionally or unintentionally, has often helped hide these vices. When a member raises an issue of defilement, rape, or assault, the church typically (though this is changing) prefers to handle it "in-house." This involves sitting down with the alleged offender, the victim, and their families to sort it out internally. If the perpetrator refuses to attend, the discussions proceed without them, often resulting in the victim being blamed. If the victim does attend, they are usually encouraged to forgive, forget, and move on, with an implicit expectation to never talk about it again.

The church plays a significant role in shaping cultural norms and lives. However, when it comes to practising justice in cases of assault, defilement, incest, and rape, the church often fails to follow the law of the land. Instead of addressing the root of the problem, the church frequently opts for temporary solutions, offering therapy and addressing only the symptoms of the issue.

In some cases, when a church leader is found guilty of such crimes, they are asked to step down or take a sabbatical leave. These individuals often set up new congregations elsewhere, continuing their predatory behaviour with new victims. The general congregation is rarely informed about the true reason for the leader's departure, maintaining the secrecy and allowing the cycle to continue.

---

[17] 1 and 2 Kings A biblical figure in the Old Testament whose dressing is often used as resembling a prostitute by Christians because of its description in Kings 9:30.

Culture and religion, while essential for providing a sense of identity and community, can also perpetuate harmful practices if not critically examined and reformed. The church, in particular, has a responsibility to protect its members and uphold justice, following both moral and legal guidelines. Addressing the root causes of sexual violence and ensuring transparency and accountability within religious institutions is crucial for creating a safer and more just society.

08

What is Wrong is Wrong

For years, we tell a girl child to sit properly and close her legs because those parts in between her legs are private and hers alone. However, we make a crucial mistake: we fail to explain the true reasons for sitting properly and closing her legs. We overlook the fact that merely closing her legs won't be enough; it's not the complete solution. While we are teaching her to dress modestly and close her legs, we neglect to address a harsh reality: some men are learning ways to get past her closed legs. They learn from society, pornography, and Hollywood to view those hidden parts as entertainment and adventure. They see it as a rite of passage, a playground and a hunting ground, theirs to explore and pillage. So, they will find ways to get those legs to open. Despite her efforts and words, they believe those parts are theirs to discover and exploit.

This XY beast will demand what he believes is his to take, will conquer because he assumes it's in his nature to do so—whether she cries, fights back, says no, or says yes after his relentless persistence, it does not matter much. Besides, haven't men devised a saying that when a woman says no, she really means yes? It is thus important to continue teaching her the value of what she has and the significance of setting visible boundaries to prevent pillages and exploitation. At the same time, we must teach males that their lack of self-control is abnormal because it is within their power to exercise it.

So misaligned are the demands of society on the female child. It dictates that we do not just teach the female child to sit properly, but to not go out at night, to not smile at strangers, as well as not to be rude or standoffish. We teach her to not be aggressive towards cat-callers because they might retaliate in anger. We teach her to be polite and gently turn down advances, so as not to provoke anger. To be feminine and accept "compliments" laced with innuendos with grace and poise, so as not to awaken the XY beast. To be sexy but not sexual. To be okay with objectification while still maintaining an air of purity. To not be a prude. We teach her to lock the doors and close her windows, to double and even triple-check her locks.

In all this, society forgets to address the XY beast. He learns to hunt with abandon, and laws evolve to justify his skewed understanding of consent. When he strikes, society recoils in shock and horror. We turn back to the girl and wonder where she tragically messed up. What did she do with her years of training? Didn't her mother teach her to close her legs? Didn't she know that's the nature of man? That no does not mean no to him? He is a hungry animal, and that cannot be blamed on him. It is his nature. Is it?

What is wrong is wrong and cannot be right. It needs to be confronted and corrected. Too often, however, the victim is blamed for the vice, a recurring theme whenever such acts are exposed. Here is a paraphrased narrative of a familiar story you might have read before.

Amon was a half-brother of Tamar. Tamar was beautiful and a virgin. Amon became obsessed with Tamar and wanted to have sex with her. Due to his obsession, Amon feigned illness and confided in his cousin Jonadab about his intentions, devising a plan together. Amon knew his desire was completely wrong because Tamar was his half-sister, but what mattered to him was satisfying his desire. When his father David came to check on him, Amon specifically requested that his half-sister Tamar come to prepare food in his presence and feed him. Tamar, unaware of her half-brother's plan, rushed to his aid, wearing a long robe with beautiful colours, as was the dress code of the King's virgin daughters.

As she prepared the food, Amon watched her intently. When she offered him the food, he refused and asked all his servants to leave the house. Revealing his evil intentions, he asked his half-sister to feed him the food in his bedroom. As she offered him the food, he grabbed her hand and expressed his intentions, which she refused. Despite all her explanations of how wrong the act was, Amon ignored her and raped her. Tamar walked out of the house humiliated and broken.

Tamar's brother, Absalom, told her, "Well, my sister, since he is your brother, it would be better not to tell anyone. Try to control your feelings." Following her brother's instruction, Tamar remained silent, hurt, and all alone. When **the father heard** about this shameful thing, he was angry **but because he loved his son, he did not do anything about it.**[18] Tamar was a disgraced, violated woman and never married.

This story highlights the pervasive issue of victim-blaming and the reluctance to confront wrongdoing, especially within families. It underscores the importance of addressing such issues directly and supporting victims rather than silencing them. Wrongdoing must be confronted and corrected, regardless of the perpetrator's identity or the victim's supposed culpability. Silence only perpetuates the cycle of abuse and injustice. It is crucial to create an environment where victims feel safe to speak out and seek justice, and where perpetrators are held accountable for their actions.

Read this full story for yourself. See the footnote.

The story of Tamar is a poignant example of how a promising young woman's life can be devastated by the sin and obsession of another. Tamar's life was tragically altered, not because of **1) what she wore, 2) what she did, 3) what she said, or 4) where she was,** but because someone else was obsessed and consumed by sin.

---

[18] 2 Samuel 13. This story is contained in this chapter

Amon, Tamar's half-brother, became obsessed with her. Despite knowing it was wrong, his obsession led him to devise an elaborate plan to satisfy his desires. He feigned illness and conspired with his cousin Jonadab, who encouraged his wicked intentions. Amon requested Tamar's presence under the guise of needing care, exploiting the trust and safety she felt within her family.

Tamar, unaware of Amon's evil plan, innocently complied. She was dressed modestly, in a long robe with beautiful colours, as was the custom for the king's virgin daughters. The setting was her half-brother's home, a place she believed to be safe. However, Amon's obsession and well-planned deceit culminated in her rape. He forced himself on her, ignoring her pleas and explanations of the wrongness of his actions.

The Blame and Secrecy

The aftermath was even more heartbreaking. Tamar's brother Absalom advised her to keep the act a secret, suggesting that since Amnon was her brother, it was better not to tell anyone. This advice highlights a troubling reality: the prioritisation of family reputation over justice and the well-being of the victim. Tamar was left to deal with her trauma in silence, seclusion, and depression. She suffered blame and a total loss of dignity and future prospects.

Tamar's story illustrates a broader issue: the misplaced blame on victims of sexual violence. Tamar's life was ruined by Amnon's actions; she was the one who faced the consequences. Her trust was betrayed, and her security was shattered in the most intimate and protected environment.

The Fallacy of Family Protection

Family is supposed to be a sanctuary of love and protection. Tamar lived in the king's harem, under the watchful eyes of eunuchs. Despite this, she was violated by someone she trusted deeply. The real issue was not the level of protection, but the nature of the perpetrator. Amnon's obsession and lack of self-control were the true culprits.

What is wrong is wrong. Sexual violation is unequivocally wrong and must be confronted and corrected. Blaming the victim only perpetuates the cycle of abuse and injustice. A sexual appetite that cannot be controlled is no excuse for violating anyone, whether a child, young person, or adult. The responsibility lies solely with the perpetrator. Preventing sexual violence is not about placing more restrictions on potential victims but about addressing the root cause: the perpetrators and their actions. Society must shift its focus from blaming victims to holding perpetrators accountable. Only then can we hope to create a world where individuals, especially women and children, are truly safe and protected.

09

The Home

The home is ideally a sanctuary, a place where children are nurtured, protected, and given the foundation for healthy development. It is where values are instilled, and respect for oneself and others is taught. It is basically a safe place. A safe place to run to for security. In this safe environment, children should learn about boundaries, empathy, and the importance of consent. It is within the home that they should witness and experience equality, where boys and girls alike are guided to understand their roles in creating a just and respectful society. The home should be the first place where children learn that respect for others' autonomy and dignity is paramount, and that true strength lies in self-control and mutual respect.

Unfortunately, for some, the home has turned out to be the most insecure and dangerous place. These insecurities, often stemming from abuse or neglect, are not only incomprehensible but are also obscured by family members. The issues are made to seem unintelligible or are trivialised, creating an environment where even the victims resort to obfuscation when asked about their experiences. This tragic dynamic is reflected in Tamar's story. Despite being in what should have been a safe and protected environment, Tamar suffered a grievous violation at the hands of her half-brother. The family's reaction was to suppress the incident, prioritising family reputation over Tamar's well-being. This response is not unique to ancient times; it mirrors the experiences of many victims today who find their suffering minimised or dismissed to maintain a facade of family unity and honour.

That is why it is difficult to imagine the extent of the insecurity for a victim molested in the home environment to find a secure place to run to. When the very place meant to be a sanctuary becomes a site of violation, the sense of betrayal and fear is profound. The victim's foundation of trust is shattered, making it challenging to seek help or believe in the possibility of safety elsewhere. The home, which should be a refuge, instead becomes a constant reminder of trauma, leaving the victim isolated and vulnerable. This deepens the emotional and psychological scars, complicating the path to healing and recovery.

The same is true of the members of the family. They are the ones the victim would have looked up to for security but instead they become a face of betrayal for failure to listen to the voice of the victim. This betrayal makes it difficult for the victim to trust anyone else. When a victim reports the abuse to another family member, they are often questioned, labelled a liar, and disciplined instead of being supported and believed. This reaction not only silences the victim but also perpetuates the cycle of abuse. Moreover, victims who manage to escape such a toxic home environment often find themselves in more abusive relationships. Their sense of self-worth is eroded, and they may inadvertently seek out familiar patterns of behaviour, believing they deserve no better. The trauma from the home affects their ability to recognise healthy relationships and can lead to a lifelong struggle with trust and self-esteem. The pervasive impact of abuse in the home ripples through every aspect of the victim's life, making healing and finding a safe haven an arduous journey.

The Illusion of Security

The home, meant to be a haven, can become a place of hidden dangers. Abuse, whether physical, emotional, or sexual, often goes unnoticed or unacknowledged because of the complex dynamics within the family. The abuser is frequently someone trusted, someone who is expected to protect rather than harm. This betrayal is devastating and compounds the victim's trauma.

The culture of silence surrounding abuse is pervasive. Families, driven by a desire to protect their reputation, often discourage victims from speaking out. This silence is reinforced by societal attitudes that blame the victim, perpetuating the idea that the victim must have done something to provoke the abuse. This is evident in Tamar's story, where her brother Absalom advised her to keep the assault a secret, reinforcing the notion that speaking out would bring more harm than good.

To address these issues, there is a need to break the cycle of silence and obfuscation. Families and society must confront abuse openly and honestly. Victims need to be believed and supported, not blamed or silenced. It is crucial to create an environment where discussing abuse is not seen as unintelligible or trivial but as an essential step towards healing and justice. Empowering victims to speak out is vital. Education about abuse and its signs, encouraging open communication, and providing accessible support services are essential. Victims should know that they are not alone and that there are resources available to help them. Perpetrators should be held accountable regardless of who they are in the family. They intelligently committed the offence hence should face the consequences of their actions.

The home should not be a place of hidden pain. The silence should be broken, and the victims of abuse or molestation should be set free. Abuse should be confronted directly, and the victims supported. By doing so, we can begin to transform the home back into the sanctuary it is meant to be. It is time to move beyond obfuscation and trivialisation and to address the deep-seated issues that make the home unsafe for too many children and adults.

Domestic Violence

Domestic violence features here as a form of abuse but will not be given the attention it deserves. It is a not a deniable fact that domestic violence in Zambia is a pervasive issue that affects many families across the country. Despite legal frameworks like the Anti-Gender-Based Violence Act of 2011 aimed at protecting victims, domestic violence remains widespread due to deep-seated cultural norms and societal attitudes.

Traditional beliefs often place men in dominant roles and view women as subordinate, leading to the normalisation of abusive behaviours. Economic dependency on male partners tends to trap women in abusive relationships, as they lack the financial means to escape. Additionally, social stigma and fear of ostracism discourage many victims from reporting abuse. On the other hand, much like in cases of molestation, when domestic violence is reported, the police often downplay the severity of the issue, suggesting that it be resolved by the elders in the family. This approach not only trivialises the victim's suffering but also perpetuates a cycle of abuse. Once the family gets involved, the woman, who is usually the victim, is often blamed for provoking the violence. She is accused of lacking submission, verbally abusing her husband, or constantly demanding finances for the family, which she is expected to contribute to through small businesses.

Worse still, some victims who make the effort to get their abuser locked up face immense pressure from their families to withdraw the case and opt for reconciliation, despite the severity of the abuse, such as a broken arm, broken ribs, or loss of an eye. At its worst, death of the victim.[19] Families often prioritise family honour and respect for the abuser over seeking justice and ensuring the victim's safety. This misplaced loyalty perpetuates a culture of silence and enables abusers to continue their harmful behaviour without consequence. The victim's well-being and rights are overshadowed by the family's desire to maintain its reputation, further entrenching the cycle of violence. This underscores the urgent need for societal and cultural shifts that prioritise the protection and empowerment

---

[19] Mulenga, C. N., (2013). Procedual Injustice: A case of Domestic Violence in Zambia

of victims over preserving harmful traditions and misguided family honour.

Strengthening support systems for victims and enforcing legal consequences for abusers are crucial steps toward breaking this cycle and ensuring justice is served. This blame-shifting not only absolves the abuser of responsibility but also reinforces harmful gender norms that justify and sustain domestic violence. As a result, the victim's plight is ignored, and the abuse continues unchecked, with societal structures failing to protect those who need it most. This highlights the urgent need for systemic change, including better training for law enforcement, stricter enforcement of laws, and community education to challenge and change these destructive attitudes.

Domestic violence continues to thrive, creating a cycle of abuse that affects not only the immediate victims but also the broader community due to inadequate enforcement of laws, lack of awareness about legal rights, and limited support services for survivors. Addressing this issue requires comprehensive efforts to change societal attitudes and strengthen legal and support systems.[20]

Defilement

Defilement is a term used to describe the act of engaging in sexual activities with children or minors, often characterised by an abuse of power and trust. This concept is closely linked to sexual abuse, which Maltz (2002) defines as occurring "whenever one person dominates and exploits another by means of sexual activity or suggestion." Ratican (1992, p. 33), as cited by Hall and Hall (2011), provides a definition which better clarifies sexual abuse by stating that it is:

Any sexual act, overt or covert, between a child and an adult (or older child, where the younger child's participation

---

is obtained through seduction or coercion). Regardless of how childhood sexual abuse is defined, it generally has a significant negative and pervasive psychological impact on its victims.

Perpetrators of defilement tend to be older, often cunning and manipulative, possessing the ability to deceive and win over their unsuspecting victims who have all the trust in them. They may use various strategies such as offering pornographic materials, favourite foods, games, or gifts to exploit the curious nature of children (Hall and Hall, 2011). Despite appearing normal, these individuals may harbour deep-seated sickness and evil.

Long-Term Effects on Victims

The impact of sexual abuse on victims, whether young or older, is profound and long-lasting. The psychological and emotional damage can be devastating, often leading to lifelong issues. Some of the lasting implications may include:

- **Depression**: Persistent sadness and loss of interest in activities.
- **Mistrust**: Difficulty trusting others, especially authority figures.
- **Low Self-Esteem**: Feeling worthless or guilty.
- **Anxiety**: Constant fear or nervousness.
- **Sexual Difficulties**: Problems with intimacy and sexual relationships.
- **Anger and Repression**: Harbouring intense anger and repressing memories as a coping strategy.
- **Dissociation**: Detachment from reality or oneself.

Research by Hall and Hall (2011) indicates that the trauma from sexual abuse can extend well into adulthood, severely disrupting normal physical, mental, emotional, and social development. The effects are often so severe that victims may engage in inappropriate sexual behaviours or suffer from various psychological issues.

Societal and Cultural Challenges

A significant issue is the societal and cultural normalisation of sexual abuse. Deeply rooted moral and psychological problems in perpetrators are often tolerated or protected by society, exacerbating the issue. Hall and Hall (2011) highlight that incestuous sexual abuse is particularly prevalent, a problem exacerbated by inadequate responses from law enforcement and a lack of effective victim support services.

As noted already, police officers tend to advise families to handle abuse cases internally, insisting on reconciliation oblivious of the gruesome effect the whole episode of abuse could have had on the victim. While reconciliation can be a good option, unfortunately, it may not help heal the wounded victim. The role of therapists is often undervalued, with traditional cultural teachings taking precedence over professional therapeutic interventions.

Marital Rape

Marital rape is significantly underplayed in many cultures, often perceived as a traditionally acceptable act. Traditional teachings and cultural norms frequently justify it, arguing that the concept of rape cannot be applied within the bounds of marriage. This justification is rooted in outdated beliefs about marital rights and obligations, which overlook the fundamental issue of consent.

In many traditional societies, the idea that a wife cannot refuse her husband's sexual advances is deeply ingrained. This belief is often reinforced by cultural teachings and social expectations that prioritise male dominance and female submission within marriage. As a result, marital rape is either ignored or dismissed as a legitimate issue, leaving victims without recourse or support. While a married man has a right to conjugal relations, just as a woman does, forcefully taking it without consent is not love at all. That said, it is equally wrong to deny the other their conjugal rights as a form of vengeance, payback, or a demonstration of anger. In marriage, conjugal rights are a fundamental part of the agreement for both parties. However, it should not be turned into rape, neither should consent to marry or be married strip one of dignity or the right to say no.

Despite cultural justifications, marital rape is a serious violation of human rights. It involves the same lack of consent and coercion present in any other form of sexual assault. The psychological and physical impacts on the victim can be profound, including trauma, depression, anxiety, and damage to the marital relationship.

Challenging these deeply rooted cultural norms is essential for addressing the issue of marital rape. This may involve:

1. Legal Reforms: Enacting and enforcing laws that recognise marital rape as a crime, ensuring that victims have legal protection and perpetrators are held accountable.

2. Education and Awareness: Raising awareness about the issue through education campaigns that highlight the importance of consent.

3. Support Systems: Establishing support systems for victims, including counselling services, shelters, and hotlines, to provide immediate and long-term assistance.

4. Engaging Community Leaders: Involving traditional and religious leaders in discussions about the harmful effects of marital rape and the need to respect rights of the victim within marriage.

That said, marital rape remains a contentious and often overlooked issue in many cultures. Overcoming the traditional justifications for this act requires a concerted effort to educate, legislate, and provide support for victims. By challenging the cultural norms that perpetuate marital rape, societies can move towards a more equitable and respectful understanding of marriage and consent.

10

Real Life Stories

While you have read some of the victims' stories in previous chapters, this chapter delves deeper into accounts of individuals who have been violated and molested by people well known to them—close relatives, teachers, and workmates. *These narratives aim to shed light on the profound impact of defilement and the urgent need for societal change.* A common thread in all these narratives is the phrase: "Don't tell anyone" or "Keep this as a secret for us." A dirty secret.

Collecting these stories was not easy; the accounts make for sad reading. While the individuals volunteered to share their stories for this book, they insisted on remaining anonymous for various reasons. Although some have moved on, the pain in their voices and the strain on their faces observed during narration remain visible. For example, Dingiya explains that she felt as if she died during the act and had to change her name to dissociate from her abused self.

Please note that these stories represent only a small percentage of the abuses that innocent individuals endure. While we have captured the majority of the stories from women, this does not mean that men are not abused – they are. Unfortunately, we did not receive as many accounts from men as we had anticipated. Secondly, we have preserved the tone of the stories as they were told, with minimal editing. Stories originally told in Zambian languages were recorded with consent and translated into English. The recordings were deleted in the presence of the victim after the translation. No story was captured from a child below 16 years of age, but this does not mean this age group is unaffected. In fact, most of these incidents occurred when the victims were below that age.

Please read the stories with an open mind.

Mendy's Story

This started when I was 6 years old. My mother used to send my brother and me for holidays at her brother's house. A young brother to my mother lived there too. He started coming into my room, undressing me, and getting on top of me. I did not understand what was happening except I would be in a lot of pain due to the penetration. He warned me to keep this a secret. This would go on every night of my holidays. In the morning, he would be so sweet to me and because I liked balloons, he would take me out and get me balloons. This went on until I was 11 years old. I was very quiet and I kept this a secret from anyone in the family except a few friends at school. I used to joke about it to my friends. It was not considered serious so we laughed it out.

He stopped abusing me when I turned 11 years old. He must have guessed I was approaching puberty. I had developed such an immense hate for him. I did not want to be in the same room with him. I could not stand him at all. I had no respect for him as an uncle. He no longer had any opportunity to abuse me. When I was in grade 11, he came to our house to visit. He was so comfortable walking into the girls' room to use lotion. I was uncomfortable with the behaviour, so I quarrelled with him over it. I was on a roll on that fateful day; I unleashed my anger on him. He was angry and, in his anger, said I was not good at keeping secrets. That was it. How could he say that? So, I then told him that if I was not good at keeping secrets, I would have told everyone how he used to sexually abuse me several times at night when I was young. That was it. The lid on the can of worms was off. This was in the hearing of both my parents and siblings. My mother never said a thing at all. The thought of her not following up on this issue made me so bitter. She pretended as though she had not heard anything. She did not even acknowledge me or what I had said. I turned to leave, and only one of my sisters came after me. She asked if it was just something said in anger or if it was the truth. I said it was the truth, and that made her cry.

Later on, a difference ensued between my uncle and the family over something trivial, and I took it seriously. I shouted at him, saying so many things to him. I was still bottling immense emotions, and I was releasing my anger. Unfortunately, he took his life that day, and he died, and I never mourned for him.

It was after his death that my mother sat me down to establish if what I had said was true. I said it was, and she said, "I remember what you said that day, but certain things you do not have to take to heart. You just have to forget and let go because men behave like dogs sometimes."

I grew up a bitter person. Especially with my mother not saying anything. The whole past has affected every aspect of the relationships I have been involved in in my life. The whole past has broken me in every way. Sharing this story with a few people does not bring the whole thing to an end. The pain does not go away. The memories are so fresh, so much so that every episode is as real as the time it happened. I remember every aspect as though it was yesterday. Prayers have been made for me, but it is still here with me. I do not know what to do. Something of value was taken away from me, and I can't even explain what it is, but I feel and sense the loss every time.

Viva's Story

I tell you this story with a heavy heart. It happened over 25 years ago, but it always feels like now. We lived with my husband's young brother who had failed to complete his secondary school because of his drinking habit. No matter how many times I told my husband to let him move out of our house, it didn't work. He was his only brother, and he thought he could help him find a job first so he would not be a burden on him for the rest of his life.

I was 2 months on maternity leave after giving birth to our third-born daughter. She looked 3 months old at 2 months because she was a big baby. She weighed 4kg at birth. At 2, she was weighing 6kg.

On this fateful day, I woke up feeling ill. I had a bad headache and I was feeling dizzy. Since I had a C-section and had lost a lot of blood, I knew I needed to rush to the nearby clinic to check my blood pressure because I am hypertensive. My husband was not home yet as he had worked a night shift. His brother was already up and sitting outside in the garden. My maid had escorted my 2 other children to school. The clinic was just a 10-minute walk from home so I decided to leave the baby with my brother-in-law and rush to the clinic. He readily agreed. I had gone for 5 minutes and remembered I had left the iron on in the lounge on the ironing board. I quickly turned round and headed back home. I opened the door and there was my brother-in-law, my baby on the ironing board, and his penis in her mouth. I immediately had a blackout and collapsed. When I came round, my husband was screaming and beating his brother to a pulp. A neighbour who had heard the noise helped me to my feet. I wanted my baby and there she was covered in semen. At that sight, I collapsed again. This time, I woke up in a hospital bed. My blood pressure could not be controlled for days as I could not comprehend what had happened.

I have not seen my brother-in-law to date. My daughter was cleared of HIV and AIDS. She is married now, and we have never told her this story. I am confused and still do not know the right thing to do. I feel sad and hurt that at just 2 months, a monster of an uncle took advantage of her. He was not reported to the police because the 'family' said he did it under the influence of drugs. He needed family help instead of imprisonment. So, he was moved to another home. I have blamed myself for leaving the baby with him on that day.

Tacku's Story

My innocence was robbed at a very tender age in our home and in school. I grew up in a home where I thought I was loved, cared for, and protected. And yet it is in such a loving and caring environment that abuses took place and secrets were kept.

I grew up in a home with 8 siblings and a loving and caring daddy as the head of this home. I suffered multiple sexual abuses that I concluded were normal. I can't remember when it started. Some events, I have managed to block out. However, I should confess that now and again, I have flashes that are triggered by a number of things such as pictures, stories, places I visit, or even in normal conversations.

For example, when I was in primary school, I was sexually abused by a teacher. I can't remember how, but I came to learn about it through a letter my father wrote to a headteacher of a girls' school I was transferred to. The letter was written to the deputy headteacher, who was a friend of my dad, seeking help. In the letter, which I found myself reading as I secretly opened it, my dad narrated how a certain teacher and other family members had sexually abused me several times. My father thought boarding school would take me away from the abusers and provide some form of protection. I have never come round to ask my dad about these abuses because such things are never talked about in the family. The family pretends to be loving and caring, and life goes on.

A particular incident that I can narrate here is one that took place in the home of family friends to our family. I was in grade 7. I am able to remember because my brother told me the details very well. My father had been promoted to a senior position and transferred to another province. Since I was in an examination class, grade 7, I could not be moved. My father made arrangements for me to live with a family (the Mwiina's[21] we shall call them) of his close friend for over a month. It was

---

[21.] Not real name. Pseudo name used

a loving family. Besides the nuclear family, there was a brother to Mrs Mwiina who lived with them. There was a young girl of my age that made it easy to live with the family. She right away became a very close friend of mine. She asked the parents for us to share her room despite there being a spare room for me. So, we shared a bedroom. There were bicycles in the family which made great fun riding around the family house.

I started writing my examinations. However, each time I woke up in the morning, I felt sore on my private parts. I would wake up exhausted, but I attributed this to the bicycle rides because they were for adults. This worsened each day, and I shared it with Mrs. Mwiina. But she also attributed it to the big bicycles we were riding. When my examinations were over, I left and joined my family.

The school holidays started right after the examinations. I started feeling horrible. I couldn't do the things I used to do. I was always tired and sleepy. My stepmother noticed too and started checking my nipples and my belly. This confused me so much because no explanation of the actions was given. I was only 11 years old. One night, my stepmother came into my bedroom and announced that I would be travelling to Lusaka with my dad the following day. My query of why so suddenly went unanswered. I slept all the way to Lusaka basically because I didn't even want to talk to my father, who could not give a reason for the sudden trip. Secondly, sleeping had become my newfound hobby. We arrived in Lusaka at night.

In the morning, I was taken to the clinic where dad's friend worked as a doctor. After the 2 of them had talked, dad went out and I was called in. I was directed to take off my underwear and lie down on this high bed. He came with a tray of all sorts of metals I cannot explain. Remember, I am only 11 years old and I do not know what is going on. He inserted this metal thing into my vagina and started winding it while pulling out something. The pain was excruciating. It felt like he was removing my intestines. I screamed and screamed. I cannot remember for how long this went on. When he was done, he told me to get up and put my underwear on. I could barely stand. I don't even know how I managed to walk out of that room. My dad went back into the doctor's office, so I had to walk to the car alone. When daddy came, he gave me medicine to take, and he went back to talk with his friend. He took a long time. I felt sick as the world around me was spinning. I threw up so much after which I felt better.

We spent a night at a friend of his again. I was so confused. No one dared to tell me what exactly was going on. I was dying. In the night, the wife of dad's friend came in and said, "If something starts coming out, let me know." Since no one was answering my questions, I didn't dare ask what would come out. I concluded that I must be very ill and something had to come out. Nothing came out. In the morning, the trip home started. My father tried to engage me in a conversation different from what was going on. I didn't join in. I was so angry with him and every adult in my life. I chose to wander in my thoughts or sleep the whole way home.

When we got home, everyone tried to be nice to me. Unfortunately, for several days, nothing came from me. My stepmother kept asking me about this thing until one day, I screamed out in anger and asked, "What is supposed to come out!?"

Since nothing came out, my father made another trip back to Lusaka. While at the same house where we had initially spent a night, I started menstruating. I went and informed the wife of dad's friend and finally saw relief on her face. So, I thought to myself, "Really, these adults, all this trouble was about my menstruation?"

After that, my life started getting back to what I may call normal. Then my brother asked me a question, "Do you know what happened to you when you travelled to Lusaka with daddy? Do you know what the doctor did to you?" Before I could give the version of my story, he said, "you had an abortion, yeee!!"

I knew what an abortion was but did not know how it was performed. "How, how, how? I was not pregnant. I have never had sex before. How can it be?"

I can't explain my confusion. My mingled emotions failed me. I was in pain; my heart ached. The room was spinning, and I felt like I was going to explode. My brother saw my confusion. He asked me to sit down, and this is what he narrated.

You know when you remained in Lusaka to write your examination? The brother to Mrs Mwiina revealed after he was confronted at gunpoint by the brother-in-law on what your friend told her parents. Daddy went to complain to Mr Mwiina that you were impregnated while staying at his house. When Mr Mwiina refused the accusation, your friend came in and narrated the times when her uncle would come into the bedroom in the night and raped you while you were fast asleep. Your friend said that every night her uncle would creep into the bedroom and you would not move at all until he finished his business. The uncle didn't know that your friend would be awake. She saw everything but failed to tell her mother. At that, Mr Mwiina was outraged and went for his brother-in-law with a gun demanding the truth. He was missed by a shot. That is when he revealed that he used to spike your glass of milk with a sleeping tablet each night that gave him an advantage over you. Mrs Mwiina even remembered that you had complained to her of pain on your private parts.

This narration broke my heart. I broke down and wept bitterly. How could a person I had trusted, felt protected in his presence and cared for do such a thing? What did I do to be treated so? Why didn't my father tell me too? From that day, I withdrew inside myself. I closed up and made my bedroom a hiding place from the world. There, I cried and I wanted to hurt myself. I felt unloved. However, each time I was asked if there was anything wrong, I said I was okay. I was angry with the adults around me who knew the truth and hid from me. I was angry with all of them. My innocence was destroyed. Up until today, my family has chosen to keep quiet. Nothing has ever been discussed. I still do not know who the other family members who sexually abused me were nor the teachers. They have been well protected by the family I thought was loving, caring and protecting.

I am now 44 years old, and I still wish my dad or stepmum would have just hugged me tightly and assured me of their support. Keeping me in the dark and treating me in the way they did to the point of causing an abortion without my knowledge of what was happening has been hard to forgive. I thank God that I am born again now, and I know Jesus has washed me in his blood, making me clean. I talked to Jesus, and he has helped me to love and forgive, and I have a relationship with my family.

Juliata's Story

In January 2019, I (author) was introduced to Juliata, a 24-year-old woman by a male friend. Juliata had a 2-year-old girl who had been raped by her father (Juliata's husband). She discovered the horrific act when bathing the little girl who was bleeding. When asked, the little girl said, "daddy did it. He said it should not hurt because he loves me and that it was supposed to be our little secret." In her confusion, Juliata ran away from her matrimonial home taking the little girl with her.

The husband refused the story despite the little girl insisting it was him. Juliata was encouraged to go to the courts of law and attain some justice of some sort for her daughter. She was in a terrible state as a mother. Society equally blamed her for the vice. Unfortunately, the courts vindicated the villain, and justice for the poor girl was denied on grounds of lack of evidence. The mother did not take the little girl to the hospital. Thereafter, the villain begged the courts for custody of the girl. It is difficult to explain or even to imagine the pain this mother has gone through. Further still, the pain of imagining this man winning custody of the little girl. While the family has insisted that Juliata returns to her matrimonial home because this is a matter to be settled by the family. She has demanded *that the marriage should end. She would like to take care of her daughter. One family member exclaimed in disbelief, "Are you losing your marriage just like this? REALLY? It's your husband we are talking about here, Juliata."*

Yelesani's Story

At age 7, Yelesani was registered by his mother as an altar boy in his church, a role young boys look forward to. He narrates his excitement then, with sadness. "I did not know what was awaiting us as young recruits. We soon started serving after induction. Two months later, we were taken for swimming by the priest. I was so happy because I like swimming and was everywhere in the pool. After some time, I found that I was swimming near the priest, who came closer to me and when we were right next to each other, he got me closer to himself, finger on his lips (telling me to be quiet), he put my hand down to his 'thing'. I did not know what to do with it but using his other hand on mine, he helped me fondle him until he ejaculated. I was visibly disgusted, but he looked at me and said, 'it remains here.' It was clear others knew because they gave us space. That was the beginning of many more of such times. He even started fondling me in the process as I fondled his. I shared this with my sister. She begged me to tell our parents, but I knew they would never believe me. The priest was an idol to them. He was holy. He does no sin. So, I asked my sister to keep the secret with me. However, she insisted that I stop the altar boy duty. I did, to the horror of my parents who could not understand why. That was the end of church for me."

Tayiwa's Story

I got married when I was 18 years old. I failed my grade 12, passing in only 2 subjects. I didn't mind much because, while I was in grade 10, I fell in love with this guy who drove a minibus I rode on to school. Although he was just a minibus driver, he had better dreams of buying his own buses and setting up his own business. I had so much respect for him, and when I did not pass my grade 12, he offered to marry me. My parents were happy too. What was I going to be doing around the home? By the end of 2019, I was married off.

My husband started raping me in the very first year of our marriage. What I used to enjoy before we got married became a horrific ordeal. Whether you like it or not, he has to get it. He leaves home very early to catch the early riders and returns home late, around 22 hours, drunk. He will force me to have sex right away. When he wakes up in the morning, I find myself in an act I never consented to. Since getting married, I have never had an orgasm. If I refuse, I am beaten and raped. He drives by home 2 times for sex during the day, and it is the worst because he is in such a hurry to go back, and his conductor would be waiting outside.

I have 2 children now and I am afraid for my life. I have shared with my bana chimbusa, who said it was his right. "He is married and it should be given on demand. That is how men are. They can turn into animals when it comes to sex. Iwe kunakilila.[22] This is not something to talk about or share with others. Every house has its secret. This is yours to keep." So, I have no hope. This man rapes me every time. I don't have sex with him. One day I told him that I would report him to the police for raping me. He dared me to go and see which policeman would agree with me. "I married you for free sex and I can get it every which way I want," he said. I am doomed.

Jenala's Story

I was a maid. I liked my job because that is what I thought I could do very well since I could not proceed to grade 10. I wanted to be a nurse but up until now, I have struggled to rewrite all the subjects I failed in. When I started working as a maid, I was only 15 years old, and I worked as a sleepover maid. The madam

---

[22.] Bemba to mean you just be submissive to him

worked as a nurse. I didn't know what the husband did. It was none of my business. However, from the house they owned, I could tell they were well-to-do. A young couple, who had 2 small children, 5 months and 2 years of age. I needed to help in the night with them when the madam was doing night shifts. I liked my job.

Months after starting, the boss took the baby to the bedroom, saying that he was going to help me. I remained with the 2-year-old baby who was not a problem when it came to sleeping. It was the baby who would only sleep after midnight. He knocked on the door at around 11 pm. I walked to the door, and he asked me to pick up the baby from the main bedroom as the baby was fast asleep. I had not been allowed into their bedroom by madam. But he said it was okay. So, I walked in, and there was the baby asleep on their bed. I took the baby and went back to my room. Unfortunately, this became the trend that week. I didn't know what to say to madam because she had made it so clear that her husband and their main bedroom were out of bounds. I had a maid's uniform which she insisted I wear all the time, unless I was going to my house when on a day off. Then I would wear my personal clothes.

Another week of night shift came and madam went, and again the baby went to the main bedroom. This time, he asked me to stay so he could show me what to do. I stood by the door. From the door, I was asked to just sit in and wait until he had put the baby to sleep. I had trusted him somehow because there was nothing he would say or gesture to warn me. He was a normal man. The only strange thing was being in their bedroom, which was out of bounds for me.

On this night, the baby did not sleep on time and cried a lot. We took turns trying to get him to sleep. He finally slept around 2, and the boss said it was not going to be good to disturb him. Then he asked me to wait a bit to give him time to go into deep sleep before moving him. He then asked me to sit on the other side of the bed as he took a bath. I fell asleep and was only woken up by someone nude and trying to get me on the back. He put his hand on my mouth and said, "Let's not disturb the baby." He pulled my uniform up, removed my underwear, and then proceeded.

When he was done, he asked me to take a shower in their bathroom. I stood shaking, unable to move. He led me to the bathroom and stood there watching me. Before I could finish having the shower, he pulled me out from the shower and forced me down on the floor. I pleaded with him to stop, but he wouldn't listen. He pinned me down and I was powerless. I lay motionless, crying silently as he raped me. He kept on telling me how I would be rich if this did not become an issue with me. "I can marry you. I can build you a house. I can make you very beautiful. I will give you a separate salary from the one she gives you as long as my wife does not know." This he repeatedly said while in action every time.

The following night, he brought the baby to the bedroom, and the same thing happened as the babies slept. "We don't need to wake the babies up," he would warn me. The whole week I tried to speak to madam, but I failed. Will she trust me over her husband, I kept on telling myself. When her nights were over, I asked her to allow me to go home, and I never went back. I have a baby of that man, but I have never told my parents who the owner of that child is. She is mine. I will look after her. I am married, and my husband has accepted her as his own. It's enough. I just told him that I was raped, and I do not know the father. Yes, I was raped. What I have gone through after those episodes will never be forgotten. I left myself in that house in the hands of that man. He made me powerless, useless, dirty, and unfaithful to the madam who trusted me with her children, not her husband. How could I ever face her? I have never worked as a maid since.

Dingiya's Story

I was good at school. I passed all my exams very well. In grade 12, I got 6 points. My future was bright. I got a bursary and went to study economics. I graduated top of my class and finding a job was not difficult. I started working for this bank and soon started seeing myself excel. I considered myself the luckiest person in the world. Working late in the bank is an expectation. Doors can be closed to the public, but work continues behind the doors.

On this fateful day, I was the last to leave. I didn't bother because the manager was one not too familiar with anyone. I had heard no stories about him anyway. But on this day, he stopped me at the door as I was leaving and led me to his office. "I just want to check something with you," he said. "Your amazing young brain is so brilliant." I smiled as I walked into his office. He closed the door. I thought I heard him lock but thought it was a mistake. "Take a seat," he said as he sat on the table in front of me. "Any boyfriend brainy?" "No," I said. "I am waiting for the right one and for the right time. I am working on my career," I said. "I'm here," he said. "Don't we make a good couple?" He asked. I didn't answer him because by now it was clear I was in trouble. I located my handbag which was on the floor to leave. As I stood up, he too stood up and there he was in front of me. "Put your bag down," he said sternly. "Please sir, please sir, let me just go. I will not say anything to anyone." "I am just starting, Dingiya, and what happens here is not for anyone else to hear or you lose your job. Do you know how many application letters we have here of people looking for jobs?" He was pulling me about to get me down but couldn't because I was resisting. He managed to get me close to the table which I thought was safe but I was mistaken. "Don't be a child now," he said and pushed me onto the table such that I hit my head so hard on the paper tray. "Help me, help me please!" I screamed. He laughed as he instantaneously worked his hand tearing my underwear and unzipped his trousers in what seemed like a second. He truly was practiced at this. "You can scream again but no one will hear you," he said and before I knew what was going on he was in me. One of his hands was on my throat and I thought he was choking me as I couldn't breathe well. My world crumbled around me. I lay there on that table motionless and up to date, I don't think the person who walked out of that office was me. I remained in that office, on that table. He finished, got up and said, "You are an all-round brainy indeed." I left my underwear in the office. I ran to the door and dashed out. I had worked at the bank for a whole year. The guard at the entrance looked shocked when he saw me and said, "I was wondering, madam, what you were doing because everyone has gone." I didn't answer him because I was visibly crying. I called in ill the following 4 days. I never told anybody except a close friend of mine. She stayed at my flat for days.

When I finally came round, I said, "I will report the fool," the following is what my friend said: "No one will believe you; you will lose your dignity and your respect; the whole country will know; this is 4 days later and there is no evidence; you didn't go to the hospital or the police; the fool will refuse, it will be your word against his and so on and so forth; do not waste your time, go back to work, and pretend nothing happened, act normally. Let's keep this between us. I will keep your secret for as long as we live. Call me each time you need to talk." She went on and on and convinced me. I was so confused. I went back to work for 2 months and resigned because it was no longer me. Everyone noticed the difference.

I decided to change my career. My father had given me a property as a gift when I graduated with a distinction. I sold it so I could start a business. Daddy was not happy, but I knew what I was doing. I never told him anything. Now I work for myself. One thing I should say is that I lost myself in that office. I tried to fight every night to get myself back. Every night I find myself on that table, and I can smell that fool all over me. I have had to change my name so I do not identify myself with

Dingiya. However, deep inside me, I get a glimpse of her. It is okay because she is dead. She died that day.

When Trust is Compromised

If a wife cannot feel comfortable leaving the father of her children in charge of them, who would she trust? If a child is not safe and secure in the presence of her own father, in the comfort of her home, where else can she find safety and protection? The father figure in a girl's life is crucial, as it significantly influences the type of man she may seek later in life. So, if the father molests his daughter, what hope does she have? Additionally, a work environment is like a second home. If it is not safe for women, how can they work? Notwithstanding, the church and men of the cloth are trusted representatives of the Holy God and considered safe to be around. If they, too, hide behind their titles and so-called robes, where can one go for spiritual guidance? Sexual abuse and molestation have significant and pervasive psychological impacts on victims, and these effects cannot be trivialised.

11

Breaking the Cycle

To suggest that this vice can be completely eradicated is overly optimistic. Our society often lacks critical research and evaluation into understanding the root causes that lead individuals to become perpetrators. While this could provide us with some solution, it can never stop the vice. The Bible says, "the human heart is the most deceitful of all things, and desperately wicked. Who really knows how bad it is?"[23] This clearly demonstrates how difficult it is to know and understand why people act in such a wicked way. However, we have a duty to protect innocent victims and ensure their safety and well-being.

As noted, a couple of times in the preceding chapters, cultural traditions tend to inadvertently support such behaviour, despite efforts to educate citizens about its dangers. Speaking up and reporting crimes to the police, regardless of the perpetrator's identity, can be effective, especially if this vice is viewed from the same perspective by society. Ensuring a unified stance against such acts is crucial for protecting victims and bringing perpetrators to justice. However, many victims remain silent for crucial reasons such as victimisation, stigmatisation, and isolation, making it difficult for them to access any envisaged support. That is why books like this one should be shared and read, to raise awareness, provide support, and encourage a collective stand against such acts.

Increasing awareness and encouraging victims to come forward are crucial steps in combating this issue. It requires a collective effort from families, communities, law enforcement,

---

[23.] Jeremiah 17:9

and policymakers to create a safe environment where victims feel supported and perpetrators are held accountable. While complete eradication may seem daunting, incremental progress is possible through sustained advocacy, education, and legislative measures aimed at protecting vulnerable individuals and holding perpetrators accountable for their actions.

Exposing the secret of sexual abuse is no easy feat, as previously noted. It is disheartening that victims of sexual abuse or assault often face intense victimisation despite the emotional or psychological trauma they go through. Even those they trust may doubt that the incident occurred. Victims' accounts are frequently scrutinised, picked apart, and dissected until the victims themselves start to doubt their own experiences.

For example, consider Dingiya's story: someone might say, "When he sat next to you, didn't that signal he was up to no good? Why didn't you stand up and leave?" It is always easier for someone listening to the story to analyse the time, possibilities, and alternatives because they are not in the moment. The expected "normal" reaction may not be possible in the actual situation. In Zambia, there is a Bemba adage, "amano yalubuli yesa ngamwalwa."[24]

In the end, more often than not, the narrative of the story could be changed as the victim attempts to make sense or sound sensible enough. In some cases, the victimised person begins to implicate themselves and see themselves as a problem. Some may end up closing up, bottling everything up, or considering themselves foolish. Yet others get depressed and commit suicide. The "mistakes" of victims are often highlighted, justifying the act with sentiments such as:

---

[24] A bemba adage to mean wisdom comes after messing up

"Are you sure you screamed or said no?"

"You allowed him in the house/room; what did you expect?"

"You should have just stayed at home."

"What did you think would happen? All men think about is sex; you were the one lacking wisdom here."

"Ahh, too bad, now you know what they mean by 'boys will be boys.' This is a man's world."

"Hopefully you've learned your lesson. Next time, don't put yourself in such a situation."

"You may have led him on unintentionally; not all guys are comfortable just being friends."

"What do you mean you didn't know he would rape you? What did you expect." dressing like this?"

Often, sympathisers of the perpetrator are close relatives or friends of the victim. In trying to play devil's advocate, they inadvertently blame the victim, suggesting they should take responsibility for their role in the attack. The family, community, society, friends, and even the police tend to doubt the victim, preferring to believe the perpetrator who may be older, wealthy, respected, or a close family member. This backlash leaves the victim isolated, with no one to trust but themselves.

Individuals who assisted in writing this book by bravely sharing their stories have noted how victims are often doubted despite telling the truth. They have observed this pattern in movies and documentaries about sexual abuse, where victims face scepticism when they come forward. Despite the taboo, ridicule, and further abuse victims suffer, their voices continue to rise. Thanks to their bravery, others have broken through and spoken up, revealing that perpetrators rarely commit their crimes just once. They grow bolder each time they get away with it, adapting to avoid detection and escalating from inappropriate comments to molestation and rape.

Sexual immorality intrudes on victims' rights, robbing them of control over their own bodies, privacy, self-esteem, confidence, and humanity. This applies not only to adult victims but also to young ones. In Zambian society, sex remains a taboo topic, making it even more difficult for victims to speak up. Any type of assault is hard to discuss, but sexual assault or violence is almost impossible to talk about with one's closest family members when it is considered taboo. The lack of healthy dialogue about sex between parents and children leaves victims unsure how to process their experiences.

Most children learn about sex from inappropriate sources like Hollywood, porn, or friends, rather than from their parents. This secrecy further complicates the ability to discuss sexual matters openly and healthily.

The Parental Role

Our traditional culture often dictates that parents distance themselves from teaching their children about sex, viewing it as taboo. This responsibility is typically delegated to grandparents, aunties, or other relatives. However, it is essential that parents take on this role themselves, as their involvement is crucial in breaking the cycle of sexual abuse.

At key stages in a child's life, such as puberty and marriage, cultural traditions often relegate sexual education to relatives or even strangers. The first responsibility of parents is to tell their children the truth. By doing so, children become aware of the dangers around them and know where to turn when something feels wrong. This education should cover what sexual abuse is, warning signs to watch for, and actions to take if something unusual happens. Importantly, parents should also explain why sexual abuse is harmful, why trust should be cautiously given, and why it is critical to report any incidents.

Historically, the concept of "stranger danger" was ingrained in children with warnings like "don't take sweets from strangers" and "don't get into strangers' cars." However, the reality is more complex. Many have learned the hard way that the "monster" is often familiar—a smiling face, a relative, or a friend. That is the reality. Today, with the rise of technology and social media, the risks have expanded. The monster is a click away. Parents need to actively educate their children or risk leaving them vulnerable to others who may perpetuate harmful cycles. Issues like sexual trafficking and grooming, especially via the internet, are increasing and unlikely to disappear soon. Silence and waiting for an "appropriate" time to discuss these issues are not wise strategies.

Additionally, shielding children from the internet in hopes of delaying or avoiding these discussions can be detrimental. Parents and guardians must teach their children to be responsible online, monitor their online presence, and understand the potential dangers. It is their duty to ensure children are equipped to navigate both the physical and digital worlds safely.

It is crucial for parents to ensure that their children's voices are not only heard but cherished. When a child expresses discomfort or reports an incident, parents should take it seriously rather than dismissing their concerns. For instance, if little Chanda feels uneasy around Uncle Pule or Aunty Mavis, parents should investigate instead of brushing it off with comments like, "That's your uncle/aunty" or "They were just playing." Additionally, observe how your children behave around certain family members, friends, or guests. Stay vigilant and maintain open lines of communication with your children.

Parents and guardians should also teach their children about appropriate touch and how to enforce healthy boundaries. It is a parental responsibility to know where their children are and with whom. Trust should not be given indiscriminately. Even close relatives, neighbours, or trusted friends can pose a risk; it is not always strangers who are the culprits. As parents equip children with the right information and keep an open door for them to provide feedback if anything happens.

The pervasive nature of sex in our culture often leads to overwhelming guilt, especially when events beyond one's control occur. This guilt, compounded by efforts to make sense of what happened, frequently results in a strong sense of failure. Our culture, society, and upbringing have ingrained the notion that when something untoward occurs, particularly due to its taboo nature, the blame lies with the victim. This indoctrination of victim-blaming and inevitable self-blame, wherein victims feel responsible for being in the wrong place, saying the wrong thing, or somehow provoking the perpetrator, makes it difficult to report such incidents. Victims often assume the guilt that rightfully belongs to the perpetrator.

The home and parents/guardians should serve as a safe haven where children can freely come and go, and openly discuss what has happened. Instead of internalising the false belief that they disobeyed their parents and thus deserved the outcome, children should feel supported. This culture of silence fosters a deadly, cancerous secret.

Parents should spend quality time with their children and earn their trust. They need to understand that their own limitations can be exploited by predators who manipulate these gaps to their advantage.

Conclusion

The end of this discussion is finally here. To the victims who have read this book, know that your story is a powerful testament to the complex dynamics of victimisation, silence, and cultural expectations. It vividly illustrates how deeply ingrained cultural norms can affect the behaviour and responses of victims of abuse.

Your experience underscores the urgent need for cultural and systemic changes to protect and support victims of sexual abuse. By addressing the root causes of silence and victim-blaming and by empowering individuals through education and robust support systems, society can move towards a more just and compassionate environment for all. Sharing stories like yours can be a catalyst for change, encouraging others to speak out and seek the help they deserve.

This book has delved into the deeply troubling experiences of individuals who have suffered sexual abuse and molestation at the hands of trusted figures in their lives—family members, educators, colleagues, and even spiritual leaders. These stories have illuminated the devastating impact of such violations, not only on the victims themselves but also on their communities and society as a whole.

Throughout the pages of this book, we have sought to amplify voices that are often silenced, to bring awareness to the pervasive nature of sexual abuse, and to emphasise the critical need for support and protection for survivors. By sharing these narratives, our intention has been to provoke reflection, ignite empathy, and inspire action towards creating safer environments for all.

While the stories recounted here represent a painful reality for many, they also underscore the resilience and courage of those who have chosen to speak out. Their bravery in sharing their experiences is a testament to the strength of the human spirit and a call to dismantle the systems of silence and complicity that perpetuate abuse.

This book also prompts a reflection on the role of traditions and culture in perpetuating or challenging instances of sexual abuse and molestation. While cultural norms and traditions can provide a sense of identity, community, and continuity, they can also be vehicles for the perpetuation of harmful behaviours and practices. It is crucial to critically examine and, where necessary, evolve cultural norms that may inadvertently protect abusers or silence victims.

By addressing these complex intersections of culture, tradition, and abuse, we can work towards creating societies where cultural values are aligned with principles of respect, consent, and human dignity. This requires ongoing dialogue, education, and advocacy to ensure that cultural practices do not serve as barriers to justice and healing for survivors of abuse. Ultimately, as we navigate the complexities of tradition and culture, let us strive to cultivate societies where every individual—regardless of cultural background—can live free from the threat of sexual violence, and where all survivors are supported, believed, and empowered to reclaim their voices and their lives.

In conclusion, this book, "Dirty Secrets," has aptly applied the theme to explore the hidden and painful realities of sexual abuse and molestation. Through the brave testimonies shared within these pages, we have confronted the disturbing truth that these abuses often occur within the confines of trusted relationships and familiar environments. The phrase "dirty secrets" encapsulates the manipulative tactics used by perpetrators to maintain silence and control, as well as the societal reluctance to openly discuss and address such sensitive issues.

By shedding light on these "dirty secrets," this book challenges us to dismantle the culture of secrecy and shame that surrounds sexual abuse. It urges us to break down the barriers that prevent victims from speaking out, to expose the perpetrators disguised in sheep's clothing, and to seek justice.

Moving forward, it should be our collective responsibility as a people to ensure that victims of sexual abuse receive the support they deserve, that perpetrators are held accountable, and that our institutions—whether familial, educational, professional, or religious—uphold the highest standards of safety and integrity. With one voice, let us confront these uncomfortable truths, advocate for systemic change, and create environments where transparency, safety, and respect prevail. Only then can we hope to eradicate the scourge of sexual abuse and ensure that no more "dirty secrets" remain hidden in the shadows.

May this book serve as both a reckoning with the darkness of abuse and a beacon of hope for a future where every individual can live free from fear, with dignity, and in the assurance of justice.

References

Adefolalu A. O. (2014) Fear of the perpetrator: A major reason why sexual assault victims delayed presenting at hospital

Available at: https://www.scholar.google.com

Accessed on 15/01/2021

Darkness to Light (2015) Child sexual Abuse Statistics Perpetrators

Available at: https://www.d21.Org

Accessed on 16/01/2021

Guinness. E., (2024). **Nigeria's First Lady slams US celebs just days after Meghan Markle visit: 'We don't accept nakedness'**

Available at: Nigeria's First Lady slams US celebs just days after Meghan Markle visit: 'We don't accept nakedness' | The Independent

Hall. M., and Hall. J. (2011). The Long-Term effects of childhood sexual abuse: Counselling implications.

Available at: https://www.counselingoutfitters.com/vistas/vistas,11/Article_19.pd

Accessed on 23/01/2121

Kibbe, M (2014) The Pot Roast Principle

Available at: https://www.psychologytoday.com/intl/blog/thinking-makes-it-so/201402/the-pot-roast-principle

Accessed on 13/05/2023

King, B. M., (2009). Human Sexuality today (6th ed.).

Upper Saddle River,

NJ: Pearson

Maltz, L. L., (200). Treating the sexual intimacy concerns of sexual abuse survivors. Sexual and Relationship Therapy, 17(4), 32 -327.

Mcquade K. M. (2014) Victim – Offender Relationship. *The Encyclopaedia of Criminology and Criminal Justice*, First Edition. John Wiley & Sons, Inc. DOI: 10.1002/9781118517383. wbeccj131

Available at: https://www.elibrary.wiley.com

Accessed on 14/01/2021

Mulenga, C. N., (2013). Procedual Injustice: A case of Domestic Violence in Zambia

http://dspace.unza.zm/handle/123456789/2348

Ratican, K. (1992). Sexual abuse survivors: Identifying symptoms and special treatment considerations. Journal of Counselling & Development, 71(1), 33-38

Tao, L. (2017) Face Perception in Chinese and Japanese. Intercultural Communication Studies XXVI

Available at: https://www.web.uri.edu

Accessed on: 02/12/2020

WHO (2020) Understanding and Addressing Violence against Women

Available at: https://www.apps.who.int

Accessed on 02/12/

www.ingramcontent.com/pod-product-compliance
Lightning Source LLC
Chambersburg PA
CBHW022021150726
47990CB00002B/752